Bible
Dictionary
for
Boys and Girls

BIBLE
DICTIONARY

for

Boys and Girls

BY MANUEL AND ODETTE KOMROFF

Illustrated by Steele Savage

THE JOHN C. WINSTON COMPANY · *Philadelphia* · *Toronto*

Foreword

THIS volume has been designed to serve boys and girls as a companion and guide to the Bible. In its pages are listed more entries than in any other juvenile Bible dictionary. Nearly 800 important Bible words are included. These are explained in simple language, accurately and without distortion. Whenever possible, historical background has been used to enrich the subject.

Among the entries are the names of the people who appear in the wonderful Bible stories, as well as the names of cities, villages, mountains, seas, rivers and places in that far-off ancient world that was destined to give birth to our spiritual life. Included also are words that relate to customs and rites as they were practiced in both the Old and New Testaments. Although many of these words may be found in an ordinary dictionary, the editors included them because they are so typically Biblical in character. Thus such words as *covenant, frankincense, parable, Passover, shewbread* and *talent* are defined. However, such common words as *lamb, ox, salt,* and *gold* have not been included.

In projecting this dictionary, the editors never lost sight of the relation of one Bible story to another and the linking of names and places. They have, therefore, employed an interplay and compounding of definitions. Thus the name Naomi leads to the names of her husband and her two sons, Elimelech, Chilion and Mahlon. These lead to the place names Moab and Bethlehem. They also lead to the names Orpah, Ruth, Mara, Boaz and Obed, which in turn lead to Jesse and King David. In this way, through a chain of definitions, the reader is led from one entry to another and in this pursuit a rich and accurate knowledge of the Bible may be acquired. The repetition is always with variation; through this repetition the Bible words are first planted, then deeply rooted, in the reader's mind.

The editors have spared no effort to make the entries of this dictionary not only clear and accurate but also provocative. Thus it is hoped that the reader's curiosity may be awakened and that he may be encouraged to turn again and again to the Bible to read and reread the wonderful stories which the various entries suggest.

M. K. and O. K.

Guide to Pronunciation

The pronunciation of the main listings is given by respelling within parentheses according to a simple pronunciation key based on that of *The Winston Dictionary for Schools.*

ā	as in ate	o͞o	as in noon
â	as in rare	o͝o	as in foot
ă	as in cat	ou	as in out
ä	as in far	oi	as in coin
a	as in sofa	g	as in go
ē	as in eve	j	as in join, George
ĕ	as in let	y	as in yet
ẽ	as in writer	s	as in sing
ī	as in bite	ch	as in chin
ĭ	as in pin	sh	as in show, machine
ō	as in no	th	as in thin
ô	as in or	*th*	as in then
ŏ	as in top	hw	as in why
ū	as in unit	zh	as in azure
ŭ	as in cut		

b, d, f, h, k, l, m, n, p, r, t, v, w, z, have their ordinary English values. **c, q, x,** are not used in indicating pronunciation. The letter *c* in the conventional spelling is generally equivalent to **k** or **s**; *q(u)* = **k(w)**; and *x* = **ks** or **gz**, or, initially, **z.**

The illustrations in this book have been reproduced by a new process known as the "Photographic Overprint." By this method, black and white line drawings are converted to multicolor by a system of transparent overlays. The process was first described in *Color by Overprinting*, by Donald E. Cooke. This is the first time that Photographic Overprints have been used to illustrate an entire book. The color separations were made by Peter Dant photographic studios in Ardmore, Pa.

Bible
Dictionary
for
Boys and Girls

Aaron (âr′ăn) The brother of Moses; he cast down his rod before Pharaoh, and it became a serpent. After the building of the Tabernacle, Aaron and his sons became the first priests.

Aaron

Abed–nego (á-bĕd′=nĭ-gō) The Chaldean name of one of Daniel's three friends who survived the fiery furnace. The other two were called Shadrach and Meshach.

Abel (ā′bál) The second son of Adam and Eve. He was a keeper of sheep and was killed by his brother, Cain.

Abimelech (á-bĭm′á-lĕk) 1. The name of several kings of the Philistines. One of these kings made a covenant with Abraham at Beer-sheba. He later renewed these vows with Isaac, Abraham's second son.
2. The son of Gideon. After his father's death he murdered 70 of his brothers, only Jotham escaped, and became king. Later his subjects rebelled. A woman hit him on the head with a piece of millstone and, fearing that it would be said a woman had killed him, Abimelech had one of his attendants slay him.

Abraham (ā′brá-hăm) First called Abram. Founder of the Hebrew people, friend of God and husband of Sarah.

Absalom (ăb′sá-lám) A son of King David. He was killed during a revolt he led against his father.

Achaia (á-kā′yá) A Roman province consisting of all the mainland of Greece south of Macedonia and including the adjoining islands. Its capital was the city of Corinth.

Acts of the Apostles (á-pŏs′lz), **The** A book in the New Testament which gives the early history of the Church.

Adam (ăd′ám) The first man. He was created by God on the sixth day. The husband of Eve and father of Cain and Abel and Seth.

Ahab (ā′hăb) Son of Omri and seventh king of the Northern Kingdom. He married Jezebel, a Phoenician princess and the daughter of the pagan king of Sidon. Under her influence Ahab abandoned the worship of God and established the worship of the pagan deity Baal. He was strongly rebuked and opposed by the Prophet Elijah.

Ahasuerus (*a*-hăz-ū-ē′r*a*s)   King of Persia and husband of Esther. He is better known historically as Xerxes.

alleluia (ăl-*a*-lū′y*a*) or **hallelujah** (hăl-*a*-lōō′y*a*)   A religious exclamation meaning "Praise ye Jehovah" or "Praise ye the Lord."

alms   Gifts or donations to the poor. The sacred law of the Hebrews specifically directs that the people give of their produce to strangers, orphans, widows and all others in need. This very humane practice is also observed by Christians.

aloes (ăl′ōz)   A costly and fragrant wood. The oil extracted from this wood was very valuable.

Alpha (ăl′f*a*)   The first letter of the Greek alphabet. It is used as a figure of speech to denote "the beginning." Omega, the last letter of the Greek alphabet denotes "the end." In Revelation, John says that a great voice, the voice of God, spoke to him saying, "I am Alpha and Omega, the first and the last." These words denote the eternal existence of God.

altar (ôl′tẽr)   An elevated place at which religious rites are performed.

Amalek (ăm′*a*-lĕk)   A grandson of Esau and founder of a warlike nomadic tribe whose people were enemies of the Israelites.

amen (ā-mĕn′; ä-men′)   A Hebrew word meaning "truth" or "so be it."

Amos (ā′m*a*s)   A prophet of the Hebrews. His words are recorded in the Book of Amos.

Ananias (ăn-*a*-nī′*a*s)   A member of the Early Church in Jerusalem who with his wife Sapphira lied to God. For this they were denounced by Peter, and they both fell down and died.

Andrew (ăn′drōō)   The brother of Peter and one of the first disciples of Jesus.

angel (ān′jĕl)   A spiritual being. Angels are the messengers of God.

Anna (ăn′*a*)   An aged prophetess who worshiped Jesus when He was an infant.

Annas (ăn′*a*s)   Friend of the Romans and father-in-law of the High Priest Caiaphas who tried Jesus. Following His arrest in the Garden of Gethsemane, Jesus was brought before Annas who had Him bound and sent to the High Priest Caiaphas.

Annunciation (*a*-nŭn-sǐ-ā′sh*a*n)   The announcement by the Angel Gabriel to Mary that she would bear a holy child called Jesus, the Son of God.

anoint To make holy in the name of God by applying oil or specially prepared ointments to the body or person.

Antioch

Antioch (ăn'tĭ-ŏk) A large and beautiful city in southern Asia Minor, situated on the Orontes River about 20 miles inland from the Mediterranean. Antioch was the scene of many important events of early Christianity: Barnabas and Paul led the young church in Antioch; it was from Antioch that Paul started out on his three missionary journeys. It was also in Antioch that those who believed in the teachings of Jesus were first called Christians.

Antipas (ăn'tĭ-păs) A son of Herod the Great. He was ruler of Galilee and Perea during the lifetime of Jesus and ordered John the Baptist beheaded.

apostle (*a*-pŏs'l) One who is sent out as a messenger. This term is applied to the Twelve Disciples whom Jesus called and sent forth to preach His Gospel.

Ararat (ăr'*a*-răt) After the Flood, Noah's ark came to rest on Mount Ararat, a high mountain in Armenia.

archangel (ärk'ān'jĕl) A chief or principal angel. There are seven archangels mentioned in Hebrew holy writings. Only two appear in the Bible, the Archangel Gabriel and Archangel Michael.

Archelaus (är-k*a*-lā'*a*s) A son of Herod the Great. He was ruler of Judaea at the time when Joseph, Mary and the Holy Child returned from Egypt.

Ark

ark The houseboat built by Noah to save his family and the animals from the Flood.

Ark of the Covenant (kŭv'*a*-n*a*nt) A sacred wooden chest covered

Ark of the Covenant

with pure gold in which the Hebrews kept their most holy objects. It contained, among other things, Aaron's rod and two stone tablets inscribed with the Ten Commandments.

Armageddon (är-mȧ-gĕd′ȧn) The place where, according to the book of Revelation, the final battle between good and evil will someday be fought.

Asenath (ăs′ĭ-năth) The Pharaoh presented Joseph with an Egyptian wife named Asenath. She was the daughter of the Egyptian priest of On and became the mother of Joseph's sons Manasseh and Ephraim.

atonement (ȧ-tōn′mȧnt) The means by which man can attain complete communion with God through the cleansing of sin. In the Old Testament this communion had to be reached by each individual through personal sacrifices and offerings, prayers and rituals. In the New Testament man is freed through the sacrificial death of Jesus upon the cross.

Baal

Baal (bā′ȧl) A pagan god worshiped in Phoenicia and Canaan. When some of the people of Israel began to worship Baal, the Lord was angered.

Tower of Babel

Babel (bā′bȧl), **Tower** (tou′ẽr) **of** A temple which the descendants of Noah once started to build to reach up to heaven. The Lord was displeased, and He scattered these people over the face of the earth and confused their language, so that they could no longer understand one another.

Babylon (băb′ȧ-lȧn) The capital of ancient Babylonia. It was a city of great wealth, luxury and wickedness.

balm The fragrant, healing gum of a certain shrub that grew in Gilead.

baptism (băp′tĭzm) A sacred rite of initiation into the Church of

Christ to symbolize the washing of sin from the soul.

Barabbas (bär-ăb′ăs) The robber who was released by Pilate instead of Jesus.

Barak (bâr′ăk) Leader of the forces of Israel against the Canaanite forces of King Jabin under the command of Sisera. Barak, inspired by Deborah, routed this enemy in the Valley of Jezreel.

Barnabas (bär′nă-băs) A devoted apostle of the Early Church who traveled with Paul preaching the Gospel of Jesus. He was a cousin of Mark.

Bartholomew (bär-thŏl′ō-mū) One of the Twelve Apostles. Also called Nathanael in one of the Gospels.

Bartimaeus (bär-tĭ-mē′ăs) A blind beggar of Jericho who had such faith in Jesus and His Gospel that his sight was miraculously restored.

Beelzebub (bĭ-ĕl′zĭ-bŭb) or **Baal-zebub** (bā-ăl=zē′bŭb) A pagan god worshiped by the Philistines. In the New Testament the Pharisees call Beelzebub "the prince of the Devils." Jesus identified him with Satan.

Beer–sheba (bē-ĕr=shē′bă) A watering place in the southernmost part of Palestine. The first well was dug there by Abraham.

Abraham named it Beer-sheba, which means "well of the oath," after making his covenant with Abimelech, a king of the Philistines, at this site.

Belshazzar (bĕl-shăz′ẽr) The Babylonian king for whom Daniel explained the mysterious writing on the wall.

Benjamin (bĕn′jă-măn) The youngest of Jacob's 12 sons. His mother was Rachel, and he was a brother of Joseph, who was sold into Egypt.

Bethany (bĕth′ă-nĭ) A small village on the Mount of Olives near Jerusalem. Bethany was the home of Mary and Martha. It was there that Jesus raised their brother, Lazarus, from the dead.

Beth–el (bĕth′=ăl) A sacred place near Jerusalem where Abraham built an altar to the Lord. There, also, Jacob heard God's voice and dreamed of angels and the ladder that reached to heaven.

Bethlehem (bĕth′lĭ-hăm) A very ancient and famous town near Jerusalem where Jesus was born.

Bethsaida (bĕth-sā′ĭ-dă) A town in Galilee, the birthplace of the disciples Andrew, Peter, and Philip.

Bible (bī′bl) The ancient sacred writings, revealing the word of God, which are contained in the

Old and New Testaments. The Bible contains 66 books: 39 in the Old Testament and 27 in the New Testament.

birthright (bĕrth′rīt) Special blessings, privileges, and duties belonging to the first-born son.

Boaz (bō′ăz) A wealthy man of Bethlehem who married Ruth, Naomi's faithful daughter-in-law. He was her second husband.

Brazen Serpent (brā′zn sĕr′pĭnt) A brass serpent which Moses made at God's command. He set it up on a pole in the Wilderness, and those Israelites bitten by snakes and looking upon this image were immediately cured. The people, however, strayed from this original purpose and in the centuries that followed their ar-

Brazen Serpent

rival in Canaan, they began to worship the Brazen Serpent. King Hezekiah destroyed it during his religious reforms.

bulrush (bool′rŭsh) A tall reed which grows along the banks of the Nile. It was among the bulrushes that Pharaoh's daughter found the infant Moses.

burning bush God spoke to Moses from the midst of a flaming bush and told him that he had been chosen to deliver the Children of Israel out of Egypt into a land flowing with milk and honey.

burnt offering (ôf′ẽr-ing) An offering to God which was consumed by fire upon the altar. This ceremony symbolized complete submission to the will of God by the person who offered the sacrifice.

Caesar (sē′zẽr) The name used in the New Testament for the ruling Roman emperors.

Caesarea (sĕs-a-rē′a) A Roman city on the Mediterranean Sea about 64 miles northwest of Jerusalem. It was built by Herod the Great and named in honor of Augustus Caesar.

Caiaphas (kā′ya-fas) Friend of the Romans, son-in-law of Annas and High Priest at the time of the arrest of Jesus. Caiaphas had sought the death of Jesus. He tried Jesus and then turned Him over to the Roman Procurator, Pontius Pilate.

Cain (kān) The first-born son of Adam and Eve. He was a tiller of the soil and killed his brother Abel in a fit of jealousy. For this, the first murder, God drove him from Eden.

Caleb (kā'lab) A spy sent out by Moses to report on the power and strength of the people of Canaan.

Calvary (kăl'va-rĭ) A hill outside of Jerusalem where Jesus was crucified. It was also called Golgotha.

Cana (kā'na) It was at a wedding in the village of Cana, in Galilee, that Jesus performed His first miracle. He changed water into wine.

Canaan (kā'nan), **Land of** That part of Palestine which lay between the Mediterranean and the River Jordan.

Capernaum (ka-pĕr'na-am) After leaving Nazareth, Jesus made His home in Capernaum, a city on the western shore of the Sea of Galilee. There He preached and performed miracles.

Captivity (kăp-tĭv'ĭ-tĭ) The term applied to the periods when the Children of Israel were carried as captives into foreign lands, especially Assyria and Babylonia, and forced to live in bondage.

Carmel (kär'mĕl) It was on Mount Carmel that the Prophet Elijah built an altar to the Lord and tested the powers of the pagan god Baal.

centurion (sĕn-tū'rĭ-an) An officer in the Roman army who had command of a hundred men.

Chaldea (kăl-dē'a) The ancient and Biblical name for the southern part of Babylonia. Chaldea was a great fertile plain watered and enriched by the Euphrates and Tigris Rivers.

cherub (chĕr'ab) A winged creature symbolizing the presence of God. Two cherubim of gold hovered above the mercy seat of the Ark of the Covenant; cherubim also guarded the tree of life in the Garden of Eden.

Chilion (kĭl'ĭ-ŏn) One of the two sons of Naomi and Elimelech. He married Orpah and soon afterward died in Moab.

Christ (krīst) The Anointed One or the Messiah. Jesus of Nazareth was proclaimed as the Christ and the Messiah.

Christian (krĭs'chan) The name given to those who believe and practice the teachings of Jesus the Christ. The name was first used at Antioch.

Chronicles (krŏn'ĭ-klz), **First and Second** Two books of the Old Testament ascribed in part to

Ezra. They cover almost the same historical period as the books of Kings. First Chronicles contains the sacred history by genealogies from the Creation through the reign of King David. Second Chronicles gives the history of the kings of the Kingdom of Judah down to the Return from the Captivity.

Chuza (kū′zȧ) A steward in the palace of Herod Antipas. His wife, Joanna, was one of the first followers of Jesus.

Claudius Lysias (klô′dĭ-ȧs lĭs′ĭ-ȧs) The captain of a Roman cohort who saved Paul from the angry mob in Jerusalem and sent him to Felix, the governor of Caesarea.

Cleopas (klē′ō-păs) One of the two disciples who spoke with Jesus on the way to Emmaus after the Resurrection.

Colossians (kō-lŏsh′ȧnz), **Epistle to the** A New Testament book. It is a letter written by Paul to the Christians of Colosse, a city of south-central Asia Minor.

Communion (kȧ-mūn′yȧn) A sacred rite of the Christian Church symbolizing man's spiritual fellowship with God. Bread and wine are taken in commemoration of the Last Supper or the Lord's Supper.

consecrate To set apart or dedicate to the service of God.

Corinthians (kō-rĭn′thĭ-ȧnz), **First and Second** Two New Testament books. These books are epistles, or letters of advice and guidance written by Paul to the young Christian Church at Corinth.

Cornelius (kôr-nēl′yȧs) A good and kind Roman centurion who, after a vision, was baptized by Peter, together with his family. Cornelius thus became the first Christian convert from among the Gentiles.

covenant (kŭv′ȧ-nȧnt) A solemn agreement. Noah built the ark because of his covenant with God. The Ten Commandments are man's covenant with God.

Crucifixion (krōō-sĭ-fĭk′shȧn) A torturous method of death used by the Romans, in which the victim was tied or nailed to a cross until dead.

cubit (kū′bĭt) A measure of length used by the ancient Jews. A cubit was originally the length of the human arm from the elbow to the tip of the middle finger. However, it varied through the centuries from 18 to 25 inches.

Cush (kŭsh) A son of Ham and the name of the land in which his descendants lived.

Cyprus (sī′prȧs) An island in the northeastern Mediterranean to which many early Christians migrated after the stoning of Stephen. Barnabas was born on Cyprus, and it was visited by the missionaries Paul and Mark.

Cyrene (sī-rē′nĭ) A large city in North Africa, the home of Simon of Cyrene. He was in Jerusalem on the day of the Crucifixion and carried the cross for Jesus.

Cyrenius (sī-rē′nĭ-ăs) The Greek form of the Roman name Quirinius. Cyrenius, or Publius Sulpicius Quirinius, was the Roman governor of Syria who went to Judaea in A.D. 6 to number the people for taxation. He is mentioned in the Gospel of Luke.

Cyrus (sī′răs) The founder of the Persian Empire, known as Cyrus the Great. It was he who released the Jews of the Captivity and encouraged them to return to Jerusalem and rebuild their Temple.

Dagon (dā′gŏn) A pagan god of the Philistines, believed to have the face and hands of a man and the tail of a fish.

Dalmatia (dăl-mā′shĭ-à) The mountainous eastern shore of the Adriatic Sea. It was to this place that Paul sent his friend Titus as a missionary.

Damascus (dà-măs′kàs) An ancient city in Syria. It was on the road to Damascus that Paul saw the vision of the risen Lord; in this city he was also converted.

Dan (dăn) 1. The son of Jacob and Bilhah, Rachel's handmaid. He was the founder of the tribe of Dan.

2. The northernmost town of Palestine. Beer-sheba was the southernmost town. The saying "from Dan to Beer-sheba" was used in Biblical times and is still used today to indicate any great distance.

Daniel (dăn′yàl) The great prophet of Israel who explained the hand-

Daniel

writing on the wall at Belshazzar's feast, and whom God delivered from the lions' den.

Daniel (dăn′yàl), **The Book of** An Old Testament book. It was

David Slaying Goliath

written by the great prophet Daniel and tells of his faith and deliverances and of his visions.

Darius (dȧ-rī′ȧs) The Babylonian king who cast Daniel into the lions' den because of his great love for God.

David (dā′vĭd) The son of Jesse who became Israel's greatest king. When he was a young shepherd he killed the giant Goliath. His brave assaults against the Philistines made him ruler of Judah and later king of all Israel. The city of Jerusalem, which he built, is often called the city of David. He died and was buried there at the age of 70.

Day of Atonement (ȧ-tōn′mĕnt) The most solemn yearly holy day of the Hebrews, both ancient and modern. It is a fast day and is observed by penitence and prayer.

Deborah (dĕb′ô-rȧ) 1. Rebekah's nurse. Deborah went to Canaan with her mistress when she married Isaac. She was buried beneath an oak near Beth-el.

2. A prophetess who lived near Beth-el. Through her prophetic powers and efforts the Canaanites were defeated by Barak.

Decapolis (dĭ-kăp′ō-lĭs) A district east of the Jordan River, ruled over by 10 cities. Many people from this district followed Jesus.

Delilah (dĭ-lī′lȧ) The woman loved by Samson. She betrayed him to the Philistines, who blinded him and imprisoned him at Gaza.

Demas (dē′mȧs) Paul's companion during his first imprisonment in Rome. He later deserted Paul and went to Thessalonica.

Demetrius (dĭ-mē′trĭ-ȧs) A silversmith at Ephesus who incited a riot against the Apostle Paul because his preaching of the Gospel had ruined the sales of his silver models of the temple of the goddess Diana.

denarius (dĭ-nā'rĭ-*a*s) or **penny** A Roman silver coin worth about 16 cents in the time of Jesus.

Deuteronomy (dū-tẽr-ŏn'ō-mĭ) The last book of the Pentateuch. It is a book of Moses and repeats the Ten Commandments and other precepts for the moral and spiritual guidance of man.

Devil (dĕv'l) The name sometimes used in the New Testament to refer to Satan.

Didymus (dĭd'ĭ-m*a*s) The family name of the Apostle Thomas.

Dinah (dī'n*a*) A daughter of Jacob and Leah, whose brothers slew all the male Shechemites for a wrong which had been done to her.

Dionysius (dī-ō-nĭsh'ĭ-*a*s) A well-known Athenian converted by Paul. He became the first bishop of Athens.

disciple (dĭ-sī'pl) One who follows or adheres to the doctrine of another. Those who believed in the Gospel of Jesus and followed Him were called His disciples. The Twelve Apostles are often referred to as the Twelve Disciples.

Dispersion (dĭs-pẽr'sh*a*n), **Jews of the** A term applied to those Jews who remained in foreign lands after the end of the Babylonian Captivity.

Doeg (dō'ĕg) The chief of Saul's herdsmen. He was present at Nob when the priest Ahimelech gave Goliath's sword to young David. Doeg reported this to Saul. Then at Saul's orders he slew Ahimelech and 85 other priests. He also killed all the inhabitants and livestock of Nob.

Dorcas (dôr'k*a*s) A woman disciple, also known as Tabitha, who lived at Joppa and was raised from the dead by the prayers of Peter.

Dothan (dō'th*a*n) The caravan route from Damascus to Egypt passed through the town and district of Dothan. It was there that Joseph was sold to the Ishmaelites by his jealous brothers and there that the king of Syria's soldiers were struck blind in answer to Elisha's prayer.

Drusilla (drōō-sĭl'*a*) The youngest daughter of Herod Agrippa I and his wife Cypros. She was the wife of Felix, a procurator of Judaea, and was present at Paul's trial.

Ebal (ē'b*a*l), **Mount** It was on the top of this mountain in the district of Manasseh that Joshua built an altar to God. There he warned the Children of Israel about the curses which God would send if they disobeyed His laws.

E

Mount Ebal

Ebed–melech (ē-bĕd=mē′lĕk) The Ethiopian eunuch who begged King Zedekiah to pardon the Prophet Jeremiah and then drew him up with a rope out of the dark, muddy dungeon.

Eben–ezer (ĕb-*a*n=ē′zẽr) The stone Samuel set up after the defeat of the Philistines in commemoration of the "help" God had given the forces of Israel.

Ecclesiastes (ĕ-klē-zĭ-ăs′tēz) A book of the Old Testament containing the stories and wisdom of Solomon.

Eden (ē′d'n) The Paradise which was the first home of man. It is believed to have been located in Asia Minor between the Tigris and Euphrates Rivers. God drove Adam and Eve out of Eden because they had tasted of the fruit of the tree of knowledge.

Edom (ē′d*a*m) Esau was called Edom, which means "red," because he sold his birthright to his brother Jacob for a meal of red lentils.

Edomites (ē′d*a*m-īts) The descendants of Esau, who inhabited a land south of the Dead Sea. They were bitter enemies of the other

Adam and Eve Expelled from Eden

Israelites, who lived in the lands to the north.

Eglon (ĕg'lŏn) A very fat man, king of Moab, who conquered part of Israel and held its people in bondage for 18 years.

Ehud (ē'hŭd) A left-handed man of great strength who slew the fat King Eglon. He then delivered his persecuted people from the Moabites.

Elah (ē'lȧ) A valley which lies halfway between Bethlehem and the Mediterranean, where David slew Goliath.

Elam (ē'lȧm) A district south of Assyria and east of Babylonia. It was inhabited by the descendants of Shem, the son of Noah. In Abraham's day this district was so powerful that it received tribute from all its neighbors.

Elath (ē'lăth) A town in Edom at the head of the Arabian Gulf. It was seen by the Israelites after they left Mount Sinai, was captured by King David, and later served as a port for King Solomon.

elder (ĕl'dẽr) The title of the leaders of the Israelite tribes and of the synagogue officers. In the New Testament the term means the same as bishop.

Eleazar (ĕl-ĭ-ā'zẽr) 1. One of Aaron's sons. After Aaron's death he became High Priest.

2. A son of Abinadab, who was entrusted with the care of the Ark of the Covenant during Samuel's time.

Eli (ē'lī) The High Priest at Shiloh to whom Hannah entrusted her little son Samuel. Eli served God for 40 years and died when he was 98, after learning of the defeat of Israel by the Philistines and the capture of the Ark of the Covenant.

Eli, Eli, lama sabachthani "My God, my God, why hast thou forsaken me?" The fourth cry in a series of seven uttered by Jesus upon the cross. In Mark's Gospel Eloi is used for Eli.

Eliakim (ē-lī'ȧ-kĭm) A son of Hilkiah and steward of King Hezekiah's household. He was highly regarded by the Prophet Isaiah.

Elihu (ĭ-lī'hū) One of Job's friends.

Elijah (ĭ-lī'jȧ) One of the great prophets of Israel. He defied King Ahab and his evil queen, Jezebel, and fought against the worship of the pagan god Baal. When Elijah's work on earth was finished, he rose in a whirlwind into heaven, never knowing death.

Elim (ē'lĭm) A pleasant oasis of 12 springs and 70 palm trees which was the Israelites' second resting place after crossing the Red Sea.

Elimelech (ĭ-lĭm'ȧ-lĕk) A man from Bethlehem, the husband of

Naomi. Their son Mahlon became Ruth's first husband.

Elisabeth (ĭ-lĭz′a-bĕth) The wife of the priest Zacharias and mother of John the Baptist. She was also a cousin of Mary, the mother of Jesus.

Elisha (ĭ-lī′sha) The prophet who inherited Elijah's mantle and continued the fight against pagan gods.

Elkanah (ĕl-kā′na) The husband of Hannah and father of the Prophet Samuel.

Emmanuel (ĕ-măn′ū-ĕl) or **Immanuel** (ĭ-măn′ū-al) A name meaning "God with us." It was prophesied in Isaiah that a child bearing this name would be born as a sign from God to Israel that salvation was at hand. In the Gospel of Matthew the child Jesus is hailed as this long-awaited Messiah.

Emmaus (ĕ-mā′as) A village near Jerusalem. It was on the way to Emmaus that Jesus appeared to two of His disciples on the day of His Resurrection.

En–dor (ĕn′=dôr) A village in the territory of Manasseh, where Saul went to consult the witch before the fatal battle of Gilboa.

En–gedi (ĕn=gē′dī) An oasis on the west shore of the Dead Sea, near which David hid from Saul.

Enoch (ē′nak) 1. Cain's eldest son.

2. The father of Methuselah. He was a very holy man and lived 365 years.

Epaenetus (ĭ-pē′nĭ-tas) The first Christian convert in Greece. Paul called him "my wellbeloved."

Epaphras (ĕp′a-frăs) A man from Colosse who was a faithful minister and friend of Paul.

Ephesians (ĭ-fē′zhanz), **Epistle to the** A letter written by Paul to the church at Ephesus during his first imprisonment in Rome. It is part of the New Testament.

Ephesus (ĕf′ĭ-sas) A sacred city of the pagan goddess Diana on the Aegean coast of Asia Minor. Paul preached there for several years.

Ephod

ephod (ē′fŏd) An apronlike vestment worn by Hebrew priests under their breastplates.

Ephraim (ē′frā-ĭm) Joseph's second son and that part of Canaan named after him.

Ephraim (ē'frā-ĭm), **The wood of**
A forest on the east side of the Jordan, where the fatal battle was fought between the forces of King David and his son Absalom.

Ephron (ē'frôn) The son of Zohar, a Hittite, from whom Abraham bought the cave of Machpelah. In this cave Sarah, Abraham, Isaac, Leah, Rebekah and Jacob were buried.

epistle (ĭ-pĭs'l) A letter. Twenty-one of the 27 books of the New Testament are in the form of letters or epistles.

Erastus (ĭ-răs'tăs) One of Paul's attendants at Ephesus. Paul sent him, together with Timothy, as a missionary into Macedonia.

Esar—haddon (ē-sär=hăd'ăn) A powerful Assyrian king who took Manasseh, king of Judah, to Babylonia as a captive.

Esau (ē'sô) The hairy, eldest son of Isaac, who sold his birthright to his jealous brother Jacob for a pottage of red lentils.

Essenes (ĕ-sēnz') A Hebrew sect which followed strict laws of communal living, self-denial, temperance, and purity.

Esther (ĕs'tẽr) A Hebrew orphan girl who was brought up by her cousin Mordecai and who later married Ahasuerus (Xerxes), the king of Persia. As his queen she was able to save her people from a cruel persecution. This story is told in the Book of Esther.

Ethiopia (ē-thĭ-ō'pĭ-ă) A land which lies south of Egypt. In ancient times it was known as the land of Cush.

Euphrates (ū-frā'tēz) The largest and longest river of western Asia. It was one of the four streams of Eden.

Eutychus (ū'tĭ-kăs) A young man of Troas who fell from a third-story window while listening to Paul. He was restored to life by the apostle.

evangelist (ĭ-văn'jă-lĭst) One who proclaims glad tidings. In the New Testament the term is applied to those members of the Early Church who traveled abroad preaching the Gospel.

Eve (ēv) The name of the first woman, whom God created as a wife for Adam.

Exile (ĕk'sīl; ĕg'zīl) Another term for Captivity, the periods when the Children of Israel were carried as captives into foreign lands and forced to live in bondage.

Exodus (ĕk'sō-dăs) 1. The name used to designate God's deliverance of the Children of Israel from bondage in Egypt and the 40 years during which they wandered in the Wilderness seeking the Promised Land.

2. One of the books of the Old Testament. It is part of the Pentateuch and relates the history of the Israelites from the death of Joseph to the building of the Tabernacle in the Wilderness.

Ezekiel (ē-zēk'yȧl) One of the four greater Jewish prophets. He lived and prophesied in Babylon during 22 years of the Captivity. He is generally believed to be the author of the Book of Ezekiel, one of the great books of prophecy of the Old Testament.

Ezra (ĕz'rȧ) A learned and pious Hebrew priest and interpreter of the sacred law who lived many years in captivity in Babylon. At one time the king of Persia permitted him to visit Jerusalem, where he instituted many important religious reforms.

Ezra

Ezra (ĕz'rȧ), **The Book of** One of the books of the Old Testament, parts of which are believed to have been written by Ezra the priest.

Fair Havens (fâr hā'vȧnz) A small bay on the south shore of Crete, where Paul's ship sought refuge before the shipwreck.

faith Complete belief and trust in a person or thing, such as a religious doctrine. The Christian definition of faith is clearly stated in the New Testament Epistle to the Hebrews: "Now faith is the substance of things hoped for, the evidence of things not seen."

fasting The periodic abstinence from all or some foods to show humility, penitence, or grief.

feasts and festivals (fĕs'tĭ-vȧlz) Joyous religious celebrations marking the faith of the Hebrew people. The three important festivals are the Passover, Pentecost and the Feast of Tabernacles.

Felix (fē'lĭks) The Roman procurator of Judaea before whom Paul was tried at Caesarea.

Festus (fĕs'tȧs), **Porcius** (pôr'shĭ-ȧs) The procurator of Judaea who succeeded Felix and heard Paul's cause before Herod Agrippa II and Bernice.

fire In the Old Testament, fire often symbolized the presence of God.

firmament (fẽr'mȧ-mȧnt) The sky or heavens. The dwelling place of God.

firstborn In memory of the Exodus

and in thanksgiving to God, the Hebrews considered their first-born sons as "devoted to God." They redeemed them with an offering within one month of their birth.

first fruits and firstlings The first fruits of the crops and the first-born among the animals were "devoted to God" and were offered at the altar.

Flood The deluge in the time of Noah. Because of man's wickedness God decided to flood the earth and thus destroy all living things. However, He changed His mind and told Noah to build

Flood

an ark and to save two of every living thing. He also told Noah to take his wife and sons and their families with him into the ark.

forty (fôr'tĭ) An important number in the Bible. It indicates a lapse of time which ushers in a new era. The Flood lasted 40 days. The Children of Israel wandered for 40 years before reaching the Promised Land. Moses was on Mount Sinai for 40 days before he received the tablets of the Law. Jesus spent 40 days in the Wilderness before His ministry, and He remained on earth for 40 days between His Resurrection and Ascension.

Burning Frankincense

frankincense (frăngk'ĭn-sĕns) A fragrant white gum which the ancient Hebrews burnt for its scent during religious ceremonies.

frontlet (frŭnt'lĕt) A phylactery, or small leather case containing copies of certain passages from the Pentateuch, worn by Jews on the

Frontlet

forehead during prayer. Its purpose is to remind the worshiper to obey the holy laws.

G

Gabbatha (găb′a-tha) The stone pavement or approach to Pilate's judgment seat, over which Jesus was led to trial.

Gabriel (gā′brĭ-al) An archangel who was one of God's messengers. He visited Daniel on two occasions, and he also told Zacharias of the approaching birth of a son. It was Gabriel who announced to the Virgin Mary the coming birth of her child, the Son of God, and told her the name which the child was to be given.

Gad (găd) 1. The eldest son of Jacob and Zilpah. He became the head of one of the Twelve Tribes of Israel.

2. A minor prophet who was an adviser to King David.

Gadarenes (găd′a-rēnz) The people of Gadara, one of the cities of Decapolis. It was near Gadara that Jesus cured the demented man by driving the unclean spirits out of him and into a herd of swine.

Galatians (ga-lā′shanz), **Epistle to the** A letter written by Paul to some early Christians who lived in Galatia, a district in Asia Minor just south of the Black Sea. This letter forms one of the books of the New Testament.

Galeed (găl′ĭ-ĕd) The name Jacob gave to the heap of stones which had been raised on Mount Gilead as witness to the covenant between him and Laban.

Galilaean (găl-a-lē′an) A native of the province of Galilee.

Galilee (găl′a-lē) The most northern province of Palestine, lying just east of the Mediterranean. It was there, in the little village of Nazareth, that Jesus lived with Mary and Joseph.

Galilee (găl′a-lē), **Sea of** A large fresh-water lake fed by the River Jordan and forming part of the eastern boundary of Galilee.

Gamaliel (ga-mā′lĭ-al) 1. A prince of the Tribe of Manasseh at the census of Israel at Sinai.

2. A Pharisee and a teacher of Paul. He pleaded successfully for tolerance at the trial of Peter and the apostles.

Gath (găth) One of the five main cities of the Philistines and the home of the giant Goliath. David, pretending madness, sought refuge there from his enemy Saul.

Gaza (gā′za) One of the Philistines' five main cities. It was there that Samson was tortured and met his death.

Gedaliah (gĕd-a-lī′a) The Hebrew appointed as governor of Judah by the Babylonian King Nebuchadnezzar after he had captured Jerusalem. Gedaliah protected the Prophet Jeremiah. He was murdered by Ishmael only 2 months after taking office.

Gehazi (gĭ-hā′zī) The servant of the Prophet Elisha. He was smitten with leprosy for having betrayed his master.

Genesis (jĕn′ĭ-sĭs) The first book of the Old Testament and of the Pentateuch. It tells of the Creation of the world and about the first men who inhabited the earth.

Gennesaret (gĕ-nĕs′a̤-rĕt) A fertile district on the northwestern shore of the Sea of Galilee. It was to this place that Jesus went after walking upon the water.

Gennesaret (gĕ-nĕs′a̤-rĕt), **Sea of** Another name for the Sea of Galilee.

Gentiles (jĕn′tīlz) In Bible times this term was used by the Hebrews to denote all those who did not worship God, but worshiped pagan dieties instead.

Gerizim (ga̤-rī′zĭm), **Mount** A mountain from which God's blessings were pronounced to the Israelites when they entered the land of Canaan. It was known as the Mount of Blessings and is near Mount Ebal, the Mount of Curses.

Gershon (gẽr′shŏn) or **Gershom** (gẽr′sha̤m) The eldest of the

three sons of Levi, who went into Egypt with the aged Jacob.

Gershonites (gẽr′shŏn-īts) The descendants of Gershon, who had charge of the curtains and hangings of the Tabernacle during the Wilderness wanderings.

Gethsemane (gĕth-sĕm′a̤-nĭ) A place or "garden" on the Mount of Olives. It was often visited by Jesus and His disciples. Jesus spent His last night in prayer in this garden. It was there He was arrested by the Romans.

Gezer (gē′zẽr) An ancient city in Canaan whose people, together with their king, were all killed by Joshua and his forces.

Gibeah (gĭb′ĭ-a̤) Gibeah, meaning "hill," was the name of several Old Testament cities. The Ark of the Covenant was kept in a city of that name after its return by the Philistines. Another city of that name was the stronghold of King Saul. It was captured by David and later became the bloody scene of the hanging of seven of Saul's sons.

Gibeon (gĭb′ĭ-a̤n) A city near Jerusalem. Its inhabitants made a compact with Joshua and thus it escaped the fate of Jericho.

Gideon (gĭd′ĭ-a̤n) A member of the Tribe of Manasseh and one of the great judges of Israel. He was chosen by God to free the Children of Israel from the constant threat of the Midianites and other hostile tribes. He also fought against the worship of the pagan god, Baal, and destroyed his altar. He thus acquired the name Jerubbaal, which means "enemy of Baal."

Gihon (gī'hŏn) 1. The second river of Eden.

2. A spring close to Jerusalem where Solomon was anointed king in the presence of his noble father, King David.

Gilboa (gĭl-bō'à) A mountain range overlooking the city of Jezreel, where Saul and Jonathan met defeat and death at the hands of the Philistines.

Gilead (gĭl'ĭ-àd) A beautiful and fertile district east of the River Jordan about midway between the Sea of Galilee and the Dead Sea. It was famous for the medicinal balm of Gilead, a gum derived from certain trees.

Gilgal (gĭl'găl) 1. The place where the Israelites spent the first night after crossing the River Jordan and entering the Promised Land. It was later visited by Samuel and was the place where Saul was made king.

2. A town in Samaria visited by Elijah and Elisha. It was the home of the school of prophets.

God (gŏd) The Supreme Being.

The Creator of the world and all living things.

Golgotha (gŏl'gō-thà) "A place of a skull," the Hebrew name for Calvary, the hill where Jesus was crucified.

Golgotha

Goliath (gō-lī'àth) A giant of the city of Gath who defied the Children of Israel for 40 days. He was killed by the young David.

Goliath

Gomorrah (gō-mŏr'à) One of the four "cities of the plain" which God destroyed by fire because of the wickedness of their inhabitants. A fifth city, Zoar, was spared.

Goshen (gō'shan) The district in Egypt where the Israelites dwelt from the days of Joseph until the Exodus.

Gospel (gŏs'pal) A term meaning "good message" or "glad tidings," applied to the four New Testament accounts of the life of Jesus, revealing His spiritual message and His teaching. These are the Gospels of Matthew, Mark, Luke and John.

Habakkuk (ha-băk'ak) One of the Minor Prophets of Judah and the author of one of the books of the Old Testament.

Hadad (hā'dăd) 1. A king of Edom who won a great victory over the Midianites in Moab.
2. A prince of Edom who escaped the massacre under Joab by fleeing to Egypt, where he married the Pharaoh's sister-in-law. After King David's death he returned to Edom.

Hagar

Hagar (hā'gär) Sarah's Egyptian handmaid and the mother of Ishmael.

Haggai (hăg'ā-ī) A minor Hebrew prophet who lived at the time of the Return from the Babylonian Captivity. His prophecies on the rebuilding of the Temple in Jerusalem form a book of the Old Testament.

Ham (hăm) One of Noah's sons. He is believed to have been the "father" of all African people. Egypt was called "the land of Ham."

Haman (hā'man) Prime minister of Ahasuerus (Xerxes), king of Persia. He plotted against the Jews, but through Queen Esther's efforts his evil plans were thwarted and he was hanged.

Hamath (hā'măth) A Syrian city mentioned many times in the Old Testament because of its wars with the people of Israel.

Hammath (hăm'ăth) A city on the Sea of Galilee just south of Tiberias, famous for its hot springs.

Hamor (hā'môr) The chief or prince of the city of Shechem and the surrounding country at the time Jacob and his family settled in that part of Canaan.

Hamutal (ha-mū'tal) One of King Josiah's wives and the mother of King Jehoahaz and King Zedekiah.

Hanani (há-nā′nī)   1. A seer who was imprisoned for rebuking Asa, the king of Judah.

2. A close relative of Nehemiah, who became governor of Jerusalem.

Hananiah (hăn-á-nī′á)   1. A false prophet who publicly rebuked Jeremiah.

2. The ruler of the palace appointed by Nehemiah to help Hanani rule Jerusalem.

Hannah (hăn′á)   One of Elkanah's wives. She was the mother of the judge and prophet Samuel.

Hanun (hā′nán)   A king of Ammon. He insulted King David's emissaries and thus plunged his people into a dreadful and fatal war.

Haran (hā′rán)   1. An important city in Mesopotamia where Abraham and his family lived for a time on their way to Canaan from Ur of the Chaldees. It was there that Abraham's father, Terah, died. It was from a neighboring city that Abraham chose Rebekah as a wife for his son Isaac.

2. A son of Terah and the brother of Abraham.

Harod (hā′rŏd)   A spring on Gilboa where Gideon and his men pitched camp before the rout of the Midianites.

Havilah (hăv′ĭ-lä)   A section of Eden said to be rich in gold, onyx, and aromatic gums.

Hazael (hăz′ā-ĕl)   A man sent by Ben-hadad, the king of Damascus, to ask the Prophet Elisha whether he would recover from an illness from which he was suffering. The prophet's answer led the evil Hazael to kill King Ben-hadad and to mount the throne.

Hazor (hā′zôr)   A fortified city in northern Canaan. During the days of Joshua this city was burned by the Israelites and its king slain. During the days of Deborah it was again conquered by the Israelites under Barak. Later King Solomon developed Hazor into a military post for unifying the northern lands.

heathen (hē′thán)   Gentiles or those who did not believe in God but worshiped pagan deities.

heaven (hĕv′án)   The firmament and the dwelling place of God.

Hebrew (hē′brōō)   The Semitic language of the Jews.

Hebrews (hē′brōōz)   Another name for Jews or Israelites, the descendants of Abraham.

Hebrews (hē′brōōz), **Epistle to the**   A New Testament book. It is a letter about Christian doctrine written to the Christian Jews of Palestine and Asia Minor shortly before A.D. 70.

Hebron (hē′brán)   One of the oldest cities in the world, situated in the hills of Judah about 20 miles south of Jerusalem. For a time Abraham made his home there. His wife Sarah died there and was buried in the cave of Machpelah.

Heman (hē′măn) The grandson of the Prophet Samuel. He was one of the Temple musicians and singers during King David's reign.

Hephzibah (hĕf′zĭ-bà) 1. A name meaning "my delight is in her," which was given to Jerusalem after it had been rebuilt.

2. King Hezekiah's wife, the mother of Manasseh.

Mount Hermon

Hermon (hẽr′măn), **Mount** A beautiful snow-capped mountain northeast of Caesarea Philippi. It was probably the scene of the Transfiguration of Jesus.

Herod (hĕr′ăd) The name of a royal family of Edom that conquered and ruled all or parts of Judaea, Samaria, Galilee and Peraea between 37 B.C. and A.D. 70. They were friends of the Romans and ruled with their permission. Herod the Great slaughtered the children of Bethlehem.

One of his sons, Herod Antipas, ordered John the Baptist beheaded and tried Jesus. His grandson, Herod Agrippa I, persecuted the early Christians in Judaea and put the Apostle James to the sword.

Herodias (hĭ-rō′dĭ-ăs) The wife of Herod Antipas. It was she who, through her daughter Salome, brought about the death of John the Baptist.

Hezekiah (hĕz-ĭ-kī′à) A king of Judah. He was a strong, virtuous man. After instituting certain religious reforms, he led his people against the Philistines, recapturing lands and cities which had been taken from them and establishing a prosperous nation.

High Priest Through the centuries, the legal head of the house of Aaron was anointed as High Priest or spiritual leader of Israel.

High Priest

He alone could enter the Holy of Holies, where the Ark of the Covenant rested.

Hilkiah (hĭl-kī′a) High Priest in the days of King Josiah. His discovery of the lost Book of the Law, or Deuteronomy, led to a great religious reformation.

Hinnom (hĭn′am), **Valley of** A valley southwest of Jerusalem, where the Ammonites practiced the sacrifice of children to the pagan fire-god Molech. To put an end to these horrors King Josiah at a special ceremony polluted the place with human bones, dead bodies and all sorts of filth. Because of this and the fires of Molech, the Jews then called this valley Gehenna, meaning "place of eternal punishment."

Hiram (hī′ram) The king of Tyre who sent his friend, King David, a gift of workmen and cedars from Lebanon for the building of his palace in Jerusalem. After David's death King Hiram also sent materials and men to Solomon for the building of the great Temple.

Hittites (hĭt′īts) A powerful people who lived and ruled vast lands in Asia Minor in the days of the Patriarchs and of the Exodus. When the Israelites reached Canaan they were forced to fight some scattered groups of Hittites, but they soon came to terms with each other.

Holy Ghost (hō′lĭ gōst) or **Holy Spirit** (spĭr′ĭt) The presence of God in an invisible form.

Holy (hō′lĭ) **of Holies** (hō′lĭz) An inner chamber of the Tabernacle and later of the three Temples in Jerusalem. It was a cube measuring 15 feet in each direction, and it was considered the most sacred of all places. This chamber housed the Ark of the Covenant guarded by two cherubim, signifying the presence of God. The Holy of Holies was entered only once a year, on the Day of Atonement, and then only by the High Priest.

Hophni (hŏf′nī) The brother of Phinehas. These two sons of Eli, the priest at Shiloh, were so greedy and overbearing in the discharge of their priestly duties that Samuel pronounced a curse against their house. They were both slain in battle on the same day, and the Ark of the Covenant, which they had carried with them, was captured by the Philistines.

Hor (hôr), **Mount** A mountain on the edge of the land of Edom. Aaron died there during the Wilderness wanderings.

Hosanna (hō-zăn′a) "Save now," or "save, we pray," was used as an invocation of a blessing. Those who were with Jesus hailed Him with cries of "Hosanna" as He rode triumphantly into Jerusalem.

Hosea (hō-zē′à) A minor prophet whose words are given in one of the books of the Old Testament.

Hoshea (hō-shē′à) The 19th and last king of the Northern Kingdom. He was a good king and loved by his people.

Huldah (hŭl′dà) A prophetess whom King Josiah consulted when the High Priest Hilkiah found the lost Book of the Law. He wanted to be sure of its validity.

Hur (hĕr) The Israelite, who together with Aaron, held up the hands of Moses during the battle with Amalek and his people so that his sacred staff might prevail. Hur also helped Aaron care for the Israelites while Moses was on Mount Sinai.

hyssop (hĭs′àp) An unidentified plant used in Biblical times for purification ceremonies. According to the Gospel of John, a sponge soaked in vinegar was raised upon a hyssop reed to Jesus' lips during the Crucifixion.

Ichabod (ĭk′à-bŏd) The son of Phinehas and grandson of Eli, the priest at Shiloh.

Iconium (ī-cō′nĭ-àm) A city in Asia Minor visited by Paul and Barnabas.

Iconium

Irijah (ī-rī′jà) A captain of the guard who stopped Jeremiah at one of the gates of Jerusalem and accused him of intending to join the Chaldeans. Irijah led Jeremiah before the princes, who cast him into prison.

Isaac and Abraham

Isaac (ī′zàk) The son of Abraham and Sarah. When Isaac was a child, God tested his father's faith by asking that Isaac be sacrificed on the altar. However, he was spared. When he grew to manhood he married Rebekah, who bore him two sons, Esau and Jacob.

Isaiah (ī-zā'yȧ) The greatest of the Hebrew prophets. His prophecies are contained in the Book of Isaiah, an Old Testament book.

Iscariot (ĭs-kăr'ĭ-ȧt) A name applied to Judas, who betrayed Jesus. It means "man of Kerioth," a town in southeast Judaea.

Ish–bosheth (ĭsh=bō'shĕth) Saul's youngest son. After his father's death and the death of his three brothers, he inherited the throne. After ruling only two years, he was murdered.

Ishmael (ĭsh'mā-ĕl) The son of Abraham by Hagar, Sarah's Egyptian handmaid. He became the founder of a great nation of people in Arabia, where he is greatly revered by the Mohammedans. He and his mother are said to have been buried in Mecca.

Israel (ĭz'rā-el; ĭz'rĭ-ĕl) The name, meaning "let God rule," given to Jacob by an angel on the night before his reunion with his brother Esau. It was later adopted by the Twelve Hebrew Tribes, each of which was founded by one of Jacob's twelve sons.

Issachar (ĭs'ȧ-kär) The fifth son of Jacob and Leah and founder of one of the Twelve Tribes of Israel.

Ithamar (ĭth'ȧ-mär) The fourth and youngest son of Aaron and Elisheba. He was consecrated to the priesthood, together with his father and brothers.

Ittai (ĭt'ā-ī) A Philistine from the city of Gath. He served faithfully in King David's army during Absalom's revolt.

Jabbok (jăb'ȧk) A stream of ancient Gilead which joins the Jordan about 25 miles north of the Dead Sea. Near its banks Jacob wrestled with the angel of God and was later reunited with his brother Esau.

Jabin (jā'bĭn) 1. A king of northern Canaan who formed an alliance against the Israelites with neighboring kings. These combined forces were, however, completely routed by Joshua and his men.

2. A king whose forces were defeated by Barak.

Jacob (jā'kȧb) The second son of Isaac and Rebekah. He fled from his brother Esau and was helped on three separate occasions by the direct intervention of God. It was Jacob who wrestled with the angel of the Lord and was thus named Israel. It was Jacob's son Joseph who was sold as a slave into Egypt.

Jacob's (jā'kȧbz) **Well** A deep spring in Samaria, said to have been dug by Jacob. It was there that Jesus sat and spoke with the Samaritan woman.

J j ... 27

Jacob's Well

Jael (jā'ăl) A woman who enticed Sisera, King Jabin's general, into her tent when he was fleeing from Barak. She then slew him while he slept.

Jair (jā'ēr) A man of Gilead who judged Israel for 22 years. He had 30 sons, each of whom owned a city in Gilead.

Jairus (jā'ă-răs) The ruler of a synagogue in or near Capernaum. Jesus raised his daughter from the dead.

James (jāmz) 1. One of the Twelve Apostles. He was the son of Zebedee and the brother of John.
2. Another of the Twelve Apostles. The son of Alphaeus.
3. A brother of Jesus and one of the leaders of the Early Christian Church in Jerusalem. He is the traditional author of the Epistle of James, one of the books of the New Testament.

Japheth (jā'fĕth) One of Noah's three sons.

Jason (jā'săn) A man of the city of Thessalonica in Asia Minor. He entertained Paul and Silas in his home, and because of this was attacked by an angry mob.

Jebusite (jĕb'ū-zīt) One of the early tribes of Canaan. David conquered Jerusalem from these people.

Jedidiah (jĕd-ĭ-dī'ă) The name, meaning "beloved of Jehovah," which at God's command the Prophet Nathan bestowed on Solomon.

Jehoahaz (jĭ-hō'ă-hăz) 1. The son and successor of Jehu in the Northern Kingdom. He reigned 17 years and continued the calf worship started under Jeroboam.
2. A son of King Josiah. The people of Judah chose him as king in preference to his elder brother. However, he ruled only three months before being deposed and taken in chains to Egypt, where he died.

Jehoiachin (jĭ-hoi'ă-kĭn) The king of Judah who surrendered Jerusalem to Nebuchadnezzar. He was taken to Babylon, where he spent 36 years in prison.

Jehoiada (jĭ-hoi'ă-dă) The High Priest who, with his wife, Jehosheba, saved a son of King Ahaziah from a dreadful massacre. They hid him in the Temple for 6 years, after which time he regained his father's throne.

Jehoiakim (jĭ-hoi′á-kĭm) One of King Josiah's sons. He was put on the throne of Judah by the Egyptians and was a cruel and irreligious man. Nebuchadnezzar entered Jerusalem during Jehoiakim's reign and put him in a cage, planning to carry him back to Babylon. He died, however, before this plan could be carried out.

Jehoram (jĭ-hō′răm) 1. The second son of King Ahab, also called Joram. He became king of the Northern Kingdom during the days of the Prophet Elisha and was killed by Jehu, one of his own generals.
2. Eldest son of Jehoshaphat and a king of Judah. He had his six brothers put to death and established the worship of the pagan god Baal among his people.

Jehoshaphat (jĭ-hŏsh′á-făt) One of the greatest kings of Judah. He was a pious man and did everything in his power to wipe out paganism and establish the worship of God among his people. He was also a great military leader.

Jehosheba (jĭ-hŏsh′ĭ-bá) The wife of the High Priest Jehoiada and daughter of King Jehoram, or Joram, of Judah.

Jehovah (jĭ-hō′vá) One of the Hebrew names for God. Out of reverence the Jews never pronounced this word; it was spoken aloud only once a year by the High Priest when he entered the Holy of Holies. Jehovah is sometimes translated as "the Lord" and as "I Am."

Jehu (jē′hū) A soldier and ruler of Israel during the days of the Prophets Elijah and Elisha. Under false pretenses he enticed the priests and worshipers of Baal in Israel into a temple and then slaughtered them.

Jephthah (jĕf′thá) A man from Gilead who sacrificed his beautiful young daughter upon the altar in fulfilment of a promise he had made to God. He was a judge in Israel.

Jeremiah (jĕr′ĭ-mī-á) One of the greatest Hebrew prophets. His words and deeds are recorded in the Book of Jeremiah, an Old Testament book.

Jericho (jĕr′á-kō) A city situated in the Jordan Valley about 7 miles northwest of the Dead Sea. It is famous in both Old and New Testament history. Its great walls fell at the blast of Joshua's trumpet. Nearby, the Prophet Elijah was carried bodily up "by a whirlwind into heaven," not knowing death. It was later the home of Herod the Great, and was also one of the places where Jesus performed a miracle.

Jeroboam (jĕr-ō-bō′ăm) 1. Jeroboam, son of Nebat, planned a revolt against Solomon. His plot was discovered and he fled to Egypt where he married the Pharaoh's sister-in-law. After Solomon's death and the division of Israel into two kingdoms, Jeroboam returned and became first king of the Northern Kingdom.

2. A grandson of Jehu, who reigned in the Northern Kingdom for 40 years.

Jerusalem (jĭ-rōō′sȧ-lăm) The sacred city of the ancient Hebrews. It was conquered by King David from one of the tribes of Canaan and was often called the city of David. There the Hebrews built

Jerusalem

their holy Temple, which housed the Ark of the Covenant. Jerusalem and the Temple were the center of all Hebrew national and religious life. Many historic events of the Old and New Testaments took place in Jerusalem. Jesus spent His last days there.

Jeshurun (jĕsh′ū-rŭn) A name of endearment applied to Israel. It means "blessed" or "upright."

Jesse (jĕs′ĭ) The father of King David. He was the grandson of Ruth and Boaz.

Jesus

Jesus (jē′zȧs) The Greek form of the Hebrew name Joshua, meaning "Jehovah is salvation." Jesus of Nazareth, the son of Mary, is worshiped by Christians as the Son of God and as their Lord and Saviour. Through His life, teachings and death, He became the founder of Christianity. The events of His life and His spiritual message are recorded in the Four Gospels.

Jethro (jĕth'rō) A priest or chief of Midian. His daughter Zipporah married Moses.

Jezebel (jĕz'a̍-bảl) A Phoenician princess who became the queen of King Ahab. She was a wicked woman, who encouraged the worship of Baal and killed the prophets and judges of Israel. The Prophet Elijah fought her evil ways. In the end she was trampled to death by chariot horses.

Jezebel

Jezreel (jĕz'rĭ-ĕl) 1. The Valley of Jezreel stretched across the central part of Palestine from the Mediterranean to the Jordan.
  2. A city in the Valley of Jezreel. In very ancient times it was the home of King Ahab.

Joab (jō'ăb) A nephew of King

David and one of his most able generals.

Joanna (jō-ăn'a̍) One of the earliest followers of Jesus. She was the wife of Chuza, the steward of Herod Antipas.

Joash (jō'ăsh) The son of King Ahaziah who was saved from death by the High Priest Jehoiada and his wife.

Job (jōb) A God-loving man of Uz who suffered great miseries and is known for his patience. His story is told in the Book of Job, an Old Testament book.

Jochebed (jŏk'ĭ-bĕd) The mother of Moses and Aaron.

Joel (jō'ĕl) 1. The name of a minor prophet of Judah and of one of the books of the Old Testament.
  2. Samuel's eldest son.

Johanan (jō-hā'na̍n) A hero of Judah during the years following the destruction of Jerusalem and the Temple by Nebuchadnezzar.

John (jŏn) 1. The son of Zacharias and Elisabeth. He is known to us as John the Baptist and the forerunner of Jesus.
  2. A fisherman who became one of the Twelve Apostles. He was a son of Zebedee and the brother of James the Apostle.

John (jŏn), **Epistles of** Three books of the New Testament written for the early Christians of

Asia Minor. Tradition attributes their authorship to the Apostle John.

John (jŏn), **Gospel of** The fourth book of the New Testament. Tradition attributes its authorship to John the Apostle.

Jonah and the Whale

Jonah (jō′na) A minor Hebrew prophet. He was swallowed by a whale because he did not want to follow God's wishes that he preach repentance in Nineveh. After asking God's forgiveness he was cast up on the shore. He then went to Nineveh, thus becoming the first missionary. His story is told in the Old Testament book of Jonah.

Jonathan (jŏn′a-than) King Saul's eldest son. He was a loyal friend of David. When Jonathan and his father and brothers were killed in battle at Gilboa, David lamented for them.

Joppa (jŏp′a) An ancient town on the Mediterranean coast of Ju-

daea. It was there that Peter raised Tabitha from the dead. It was also in Joppa that Peter had a vision.

Jordan (jôr′dan) The main river of Palestine. It rises in the mountains of Lebanon and winds its way southward, passing through the Sea of Galilee and emptying into the Dead Sea. It was the scene of many important events in both the Old and New Testaments. It was at the River Jordan that Jesus was baptized.

Joseph (jō′zaf) 1. One of the sons of Jacob and Rachel. His jealous brothers sold him as a slave into Egypt, where he won the Pharaoh's friendship. He later saved his father and brothers and all their families from famine.

2. The husband of Mary, the mother of Jesus.

Joseph (jō′zaf) **of Arimathaea** (ăr-ĭ-ma-thē′a) A man who, together with the Rabbi Nicodemus, buried Jesus in the new tomb in his garden.

Joshua (jŏsh′ū-a) The son of Nun of the tribe of Ephraim. He was born in Egypt and he helped Moses lead the Israelites during the Wilderness wanderings. After the death of Moses he led his people in their first conquests in Canaan. The sixth book of the Old Testament, the Book of Joshua, tells his story.

Josiah (jō-sī′à) A good king of Judah. He came to the throne when he was only 8 years old. It was during his reign that the lost Book of the Law was found. This led to a great religious reformation.

Jotham (jō′thàm) 1. The youngest son of Gideon.

2. The son of King Uzziah and Jerushah. He acted as regent for his father, who was sick with leprosy.

Jubilee, year of It was ordered in Mosaic Law that the fiftieth year coming at the completion of 7 Sabbatical years was to be held as a year of Jubilee. That Jubilee year was never observed, and the Babylonian Captivity was believed by many in ancient times to have been God's punishment to Israel for this sin.

Judaea (jōō-dē′à) The most southern province of Palestine during the time of Jesus.

Judah (jōō′dà) 1. Jacob's fourth son. Founder of the largest of the Twelve Tribes of Israel.

2. The name given to the southern district of Palestine inhabited by the Tribe of Judah. This general section was known, at one period, as the Kingdom of Judah, and later as Judaea.

Judas (jōō′dàs) 1. The man with whom Paul lived in Damascus

after his miraculous conversion. His house was on "the street which is called Straight."

2. A leader in the Jerusalem church who went with Paul and Barnabas to visit the church at Antioch.

Judas Iscariot (jōō′dàs ĭs-kăr′ĭ-àt) One of the Twelve Apostles. It was he who betrayed Jesus to His enemies for 30 pieces of silver.

Judas (jōō′dàs) **of Galilee** (găl′ĭ-lē) Also known as Judas the Gaulonite. The leader of a heroic Jewish revolt against the Roman oppressors about A.D. 6.

Jude (jōōd) According to the Gospels of Matthew and Mark, Jude was a brother of the Apostle James and a son of Mary and Joseph. He is, therefore, believed to have been one of the brothers of Jesus. Some also believe he was one of the Twelve Apostles, otherwise known as Lebbaeus or Thaddaeus. He is credited with having written the Epistle of Jude, a New Testament book.

judge As used in the Old Testament, this word means "ruler" or "defender" of the Israelites against their oppressors. The judges were men sent by God to help protect His chosen people. The Book of Judges tells the stories of many of these leaders.

Judgment Seat

judgment (jŭj′m*a*nt) **seat** The chair or bench where the proper authority, such as a governor, judge, or procurator, sat to hear cases and pronounce verdicts. Judgment seats were commonly used by both the ancient Hebrews and the Romans. Pontius Pilate sat upon a judgment seat when he tried Jesus.

Judith (jōō′dĭth) A wife of Esau.

Kadesh (kā′dĕsh) and **Kadesh–barnea** (kā′dĕsh=bär′nē-*a*) An oasis in the Wilderness of Zin, where the Israelites camped during their wanderings. It was there that Moses' sister, Miriam, was buried.

Kedar (kē′dẽr) The second son of Ishmael and the grandson of Hagar and Abraham. He was the founder of a large Arabian tribe that was known for its flocks and its black tents. These tents are mentioned in the Song of Solomon.

Kedesh (kē′dĕsh) A holy place in northern Palestine. It was the home of Barak and the place where he and Deborah gathered together their forces to fight the Canaanites under Sisera.

Kenites (kē′nīts) A wandering or gypsylike tribe of metal workers that befriended the Israelites during the Wilderness wanderings. These people were related to the Midianites. Hobab, the brother-in-law of Moses, was a Kenite.

Kerioth (kĭr′ĭ-ŏth) A town in southern Judaea which is said to have been the birthplace of Judas Iscariot.

Keturah (k*a*-tū′r*a*) The woman whom Abraham married after the death of Sarah.

Kibroth–hattaavah (kĭb′rŏth=h*a*-tā′*a*-v*a*) The wilderness place

Arab Tents (see Kedar)

where God sent the Israelites great numbers of quail because they had grown tired of eating manna. However, He then smote the Israelites with a plague as a punishment for having complained about the manna.

Kidron (kĭd'rŏn) or **Cedron** (sē'drăn) A small valley or ravine lying between Jerusalem and the Mount of Olives. King David fled across this valley during the rebellion of Absalom. Centuries later Jesus crossed this same valley on his way to the Garden of Gethsemane.

Kings, First and Second Books of Two books of the Old Testament. They contain the 400-year history of the Israelites from the death of King David to the fall of the Kingdom of Judah and the desolation of Jerusalem by Nebuchadnezzar. They conclude with the release of King Jehoiachin from prison in Babylon after 36 years of captivity.

Kirjath–jearim (kĭr-jăth=jē'a-rĭm) A small town on the road between Jerusalem and Joppa. It was there that the Ark of the Covenant rested for 20 years before David moved it into Jerusalem.

Kish (kĭsh) A member of the Tribe of Benjamin. He was the father of King Saul.

Kishon (kī'shŏn) A river in north-

ern Palestine. Near its banks the Canaanite, Sisera, and his forces were defeated by Barak and Deborah. It was also on the banks of the River Kishon that the Prophet Elijah slew the priests of the pagan god Baal.

Kohath (kō'hăth) The second of the three sons of Levi and the grandfather of Moses and Aaron. He lived for 133 years.

Korah (kō'ra) 1. The third son of Esau.
2. One of the grandsons of Kohath and a great-grandson of Levi. During the Wilderness wanderings, he led a revolt against Moses and Aaron. As a punishment for this, he and his followers were swallowed by an earthquake.

Laban (lā'băn) The son of Bethuel and brother of Rebekah. He was the father of Rachel and Leah; through their marriages he became the father-in-law of Jacob.

Lachish (lā'kĭsh) A fortified city in southern Judah which belonged to the Amorites. Joshua hanged the king of Lachish and four other kings from the trees of Makkedah following the battle when "the sun stood still."

Lahai–roi (la-hī'=roi) The well near Beer-sheba where God appeared to Hagar when she was fleeing from her jealous mistress, Sarah.

Lamech (lā′mĕk) 1. The fifth direct descendant of Cain. He was the husband of Adah and Zillah. His three sons, Jabal, Jubal and Tubal-cain, were the first inventors of useful implements. Tubal-cain invented the sword.

2. Noah's father.

Lamentations (lăm-ȧn-tā′shȧnz) One of the books of the Old Testament. It consists of 5 poems or songs of mourning for the sufferings of the people of Judah at the time of the fall of Jerusalem and the destruction of the Temple by Nebuchadnezzar. The Prophet Jeremiah is credited with having written the first four of these poems.

Laodicea (lā-ŏd-ĭ-sē′ȧ) A city in Asia Minor situated close to the Mediterranean about 50 miles southwest of Antioch. It was the site of one of the "seven churches of Asia." In his Epistle to the Colossians, Paul sent greetings to the Christians of Laodicea.

Lapidoth (lăp′ĭ-dŏth) The husband of the prophetess Deborah.

laver (lā′vĕr) A brass bowl containing water which was used by the Hebrew priests to wash their hands and feet before offering sacrifices. It stood near the altar. Lavers were first used in the Tabernacle and later in the Temple.

Law In the Bible this term refers

Laver

to the "will of God" and to the Mosaic Law as contained in the Pentateuch.

laying on of hands An act of blessing or benediction.

Laying on of Hands

Lazarus (lăz′a-ras) A friend of Jesus and the brother of Martha and Mary of Bethany. Jesus raised Lazarus from the dead after he had lain four days in the tomb.

Leah (lē′a) The daughter of Laban and sister of Rachel. She had very poor eyesight and her father, fearing that no one would marry her, tricked Jacob into taking her as his wife instead of beautiful Rachel, whom he truly loved. Jacob grew to hate Leah and later married Rachel. Four of Leah's sons, Reuben, Simeon, Levi and Judah, became the founders of four of the Twelve Tribes of Israel. Leah was buried in the cave at Machpelah beside Sarah and Abraham.

Lebanon (lĕb′a-nan) A mountain range in the northern part of Palestine famous for the cedars which grew on its slopes. Lebanon means "white" and was probably applied to these mountains because of their snow-covered peaks and white limestone cliffs.

Lehi (lē′hī) The place where Samson slew a thousand Philistines with the jawbone of an ass.

leper (lĕp′ẽr) A person suffering from an incurable skin disease called leprosy. In Bible times this disease was erroneously believed to be both highly contagious and hereditary. Those af-

flicted were driven out of the community and were forced to wander through the land as outcasts. Jesus cured many of these unfortunate people.

Levi (lē′vī) Jacob's third son by Leah. He was the founder of one of the Twelve Tribes of Israel.

leviathan (lĭ-vī′a-than) The word used in the Old Testament in referring to crocodiles and whales. It means "huge monster."

Leviathan

Levites (lē′vīts) Those who belonged to the Tribe of Levi. It was from this tribe that the priests and teachers of Israel were chosen after the time of the Exodus. Miriam, Moses and Aaron were Levites.

Leviticus (lĭ-vĭt′ĭ-kas) The third book of the Pentateuch. It is so called because it deals with the duties of the Levites as priests and religious teachers of the Israelites.

Linus (lī′nas) A Christian at Rome who was a friend of Paul and Timothy. He is believed to have

Lord's Supper

succeeded Paul and Peter as bishop of Rome.

Lois (lō′ĭs) Timothy's grandmother, a woman of great faith.

Lord When this word is written in capitals in the Bible it means "God" or "Jehovah." At all other times it means simply "master."

Lord's Day The first day of the week, at which time the early Christians gathered to worship. . This day was chosen because Jesus rose from the dead on the first day of the week and exactly a week later appeared to His disciples in Jerusalem.

Lord's Prayer, The The prayer that Jesus taught His disciples and the multitude as He delivered the Sermon on the Mount.

Lord's Supper The Sacrament of Holy Communion, instituted by Jesus when He and His apostles met together to celebrate the Passover on the night before the Crucifixion. At this parting He gave His apostles bread to eat and wine to drink, in remembrance of Him. This has since become a Christian symbol of faith and a reminder of the leading truths of the Gospel.

Lot (lŏt) The son of Haran and nephew of Abraham. He was born in Ur of the Chaldees and migrated into Canaan with Abraham and his people. Because of

Abraham's intervention, God saved Lot and his family from the destruction of Sodom.

Lucius (lū'shĭ-*a*s) A man from Cyrene who went to Antioch after the stoning of Stephen to preach the teachings of Jesus.

Luke (lūk) A doctor from Antioch who was an early Christian and Paul's companion on his Second and Third Missionary Journeys. The Third Gospel, the Gospel of Luke, is ascribed to him.

Lycaonia (lĭk-ā-ō'nĭ-*a*) A desert-like district of Asia Minor visited by Paul on three separate occasions.

Lydda (lĭd'*a*) A very ancient town between Jerusalem and Joppa, where Paul healed Aeneas, a man who was sick with palsy.

Lydia (lĭd'ĭ-*a*) A wealthy woman of Thyatira in western Asia Minor. She became Paul's first European convert and for a time he was a guest in her home.

Lystra (lĭs'tr*a*) A city in Lycaonia in Asia Minor, the home of Timothy. It was there that Paul was offered divine honors because he had cured a cripple and there that he was later stoned.

M

Maacah (mā'*a*-k*a*) One of King David's wives and the mother of his son Absalom.

Maccabees (măk'*a*-bēz) A family

of priestly descent that freed the land of Israel from Syria and its pagan worship. The Maccabees ruled from 166 B.C. to 63 B.C., when the Romans conquered the land. From 63 B.C. to 37 B.C. they ruled as High Priests. In 37 B.C. Herod the Great came to power.

Macedonia (măs-ĭ-dō'nĭ-*a*) A country bordering on northern Greece. Paul carried the Gospel to this land after having a vision of a man from Macedonia beckoning him to come to preach to his people. Silas and Timothy also preached there. Three of Paul's epistles were written to churches in Macedonia.

Machir (mā'kĭr) 1. The eldest son of Manasseh and grandson of Joseph. He was the founder of a warlike people who conquered Gilead.

2. The son of Ammiel, a shiek of lands east of the Jordan. He gave refuge to Jonathan's son Mephibosheth and brought supplies to King David during Absalom's revolt.

Magdala (măg'd*a*-l*a*) A town on the western shore of the Sea of Galilee. It was the home of Mary Magdalene.

Magog (mā'gŏg) A country mentioned in the Book of Ezekiel. Its prince was called Gog.

Mahanaim (mā-h*a*-nā'ĭm) A town

east of the Jordan, where Jacob met "the angels of God." Centuries later King David found refuge there during Absalom's revolt.

Mahlon (mä′lŏn) One of Naomi's sons and Ruth's first husband.

Makkedah (mă-kē′då) The place where Joshua hanged the five kings who had escaped from the battle where "the sun stood still."

Malachi (măl′å-kī) A prophet of Israel. He is the author of the last book of the Old Testament.

Malchus (măl′kås) One of the High Priest's servants. Peter cut off Malchus' ear with a sword the night Jesus was arrested by the Romans in the Garden of Gethsemane.

mammon (măm′ån) A word used in the New Testament to denote the evil of placing too much value on material wealth.

Mamre (măm′rĭ) An Amorite friend of Abraham. It was in the shade of Mamre's oak trees that Abraham dwelt between the time he lived in Beth-el and Beer-sheba.

Manaen (măn′å-ĕn) A teacher and prophet in the church at Antioch at the time Paul and Barnabas were chosen as missionaries. He is believed to have been a foster brother of Herod Antipas.

Manasseh (må-năs′ĕ) 1. Joseph's eldest son by his Egyptian wife Asenath. He was adopted into the family by the aged Jacob and made head of a tribe.

2. A king of Judah, the son and successor of Hezekiah. He came to the throne when he was only 12 years old. During his 55-year reign he encouraged the worship of pagan gods. However, he repented before his death and restored God's altar in Jerusalem.

manger (mān′jĕr) A trough from which horses and cattle eat their

Jesus in the Manger

feed. According to the Gospel of Luke, the infant Jesus was laid in the manger of the stable where He was born.

manna (măn′à) The food which God rained from heaven upon the Israelites during their Wilderness wanderings.

Manoah (mà-nō′à) The father of Samson.

Mara (mä′rà) A word meaning "sad" or "bitter." Naomi adopted this as her name when she returned to Bethlehem, with her daughter-in-law Ruth, after her husband and two sons had died.

Marah (mä′rà) A place in the Wilderness where the thirsty Israelites found a spring of bitter-tasting water. However, the Lord showed Moses how to sweeten this spring by casting in a certain tree. Marah means "bitterness."

Mark (märk) One of the Evangelists, a cousin of Barnabas and an intimate friend of Paul. His Jewish name was John. He was the author of the Gospel of Mark.

Mars' (märz) **Hill** Also known as the Areopagus. A hill near the Acropolis in Athens dedicated to Mars, the Greek god of war. It was there that Paul delivered his famous address to the men of Athens.

Martha (är′thà) The sister of Lazarus and Mary of Bethany. Jesus was their devoted friend.

Mary Magdalene (mâr′ĭ măg′dà-lēn) A woman from Magdala whom Jesus cured of a serious illness. She became one of Jesus' most devoted followers and was one of the two women who found the tomb empty on the Resurrection morning.

Mary (mâr′ĭ) **of Bethany** (bĕth′à-nĭ) The sister of Martha and Lazarus. It was she who anointed Jesus in the house of Simon the Leper.

Mary (mâr′ĭ) **of Rome** (rōm) A Roman Christian who was greeted by Paul in his Epistle to the Romans because she had worked so hard and with so much devotion for him.

Mary (mâr′ĭ) **the mother of Mark** (märk) A wealthy woman in whose home the early Christians of Jerusalem met. She was probably the aunt of Barnabas.

Mary (mâr′ĭ) **the Virgin** Wife of Joseph and mother of Jesus. She was related to Elisabeth, mother of John the Baptist. The Angel Gabriel announced to Mary that she would become the mother of the Son of God.

Massah (măs′à) A place near Mount Sinai where Moses brought forth water by striking a rock with his rod. He did this when the Israelites began to complain because of thirst and thus

Mary the Virgin

tempted God. The word Massah means "temptation."

Matthew (măth'ū) One of the Twelve Apostles. His original name was Levi, and he was a tax collector. He took the name of Matthew when he joined Jesus.

He is credited by many as being the author of the Gospel of Matthew.

Matthias (má-thī'ás) The devoted disciple of Jesus who was chosen to take the place of Judas Iscariot.

Media (mē'dĭ-á) A powerful country south of the Caspian Sea. Its people, the Medes, often invaded and conquered their neighbors.

Megiddo (mĭ-gĭd'ō) An ancient and important city of Canaan. Joshua defeated its king, and the song of Deborah tells the story of the great battle which took place there between the forces of Sisera and Barak. Later, Josiah was slain in Megiddo.

Melchizedek (měl-kĭz'á-děk) King of Salem (perhaps Jerusalem) and

Writing on the Wall (see Mene)

High Priest of God. He met Abraham in the Valley of Shaveh and, bringing out bread and wine, blessed him.

Melita (mĕl′ĭ-tȧ) The modern island of Malta. It was the scene of Paul's shipwreck.

Memphis (mĕm′fĭs) A city of ancient Egypt. Its site is about 9 miles south of modern Cairo and 5 miles from the great Pyramids.

Menahem (mĕn′ȧ-hĕm) An evil king of the Northern Kingdom. He came to power by slaying the usurper Shallum.

Mene (mē′nĭ) The first word of MENE, MENE, TEKEL, UPHARSIN, the mysterious writing on the wall which Daniel explained for King Belshazzar. It means "God hath numbered thy kingdom, and finished it. Thou are weighed in the balances, and art found wanting. Thy kingdom is divided, and given to the Medes and Persians."

Mephibosheth (mĭ-fĭb′ō-shĕth) 1. One of Saul's sons. He was surrendered by David to the Gibeonites, who sacrificed him to raise the famine from which their land was suffering.

2. Son of Jonathan and grandson of Saul. When only five years old he became lame in both legs. Many years later, after Absalom's revolt, King David showed kindness to him in Jonathan's memory.

Merari (mĭ-rā′rī) The third son of Levi and head of one of the three divisions of the Tribe of Levi.

mercy seat The solid gold lid of the Ark of the Covenant above which hovered two cherubim. It was thought of as God's throne, from which He would hear prayers and give comfort.

Mercy Seat

Merom (mē′rŏm), **the waters of** A lake formed by the River Jordan 11 miles north of the Sea of Galilee. It was there that Joshua defeated the forces of the northern Canaanite kings under the command of King Jabin.

Mesha (mē′shȧ) A king of Moab who ruled in the days of King Ahab of the Northern Kingdom. During a war with Israel, he gave his first-born son as a burnt offering to the fire-god Chemosh in return for victory.

Meshach (mē′shăk) The Chaldean name of one of Daniel's three companions who miraculously went through the fiery furnace. The other two were Shadrach and Abed-nego.

Meshech (mē′shĕk) A son of Japheth and grandson of Noah. He was the founder of a warlike people who were allies of Prince Gog of Magog.

Mesopotamia (mĕs-ō-pō-tā′mĭ-a) The land which lies between the Rivers Tigris and Euphrates. Nahor and his family settled there after leaving Ur of the Chaldees; it was also the home of Bethuel and Laban. It was to this place that Abraham sent his servants to find a wife for his son Isaac.

Messiah (ma-sī′a) Messiah means the same as the Anointed One, the Deliverer, the Christ.

Methuselah (mĭ-thū′za-la) The son of Enoch and the father of Lamech. He lived to be 969 years of age.

Micah (mī′ka) A minor prophet who lived in the days of the Prophet Isaiah. He is credited with being the author of the Old Testament book, the Book of Micah.

Michael (mī′kā-ĕl) The name of a chief angel or archangel, who

once served as the guardian of the Israelites against the pagan ideas of Persia and Greece. Another time he led the angels in heaven in a war against the Devil. The Devil lost and was "cast out into the earth."

Michael the Archangel

Michal (mī′kal) Saul's younger daughter and one of King David's wives.

Midian (mĭd′ĭ-an) A son of Abraham and Keturah, and the founder of the Midianites, a wandering Arabian tribe that inhabited the deserts of Arabia south of Moab. Moses found refuge among these people when he fled from Egypt after slaying an Egyptian who

Molten Sea

was beating an Israelite. In Midian he married Zipporah, the daughter of a Midian priest.

Milcah (mĭl′kȧ) The daughter of Haran, sister of Lot and wife of Nahor, Abraham's brother. She bore 8 children, including Bethuel. Through him she became the grandmother of Rebekah, Isaac's wife.

Miletus (mī-lē′tȧs) A city on the Aegean coast of Asia Minor. It was visited by Paul at the end of his Third Missionary Journey and here he delivered his touching farewell message to the Christians of Asia Minor.

Miriam (mĭr′ĭ-ȧm) The sister of Moses and Aaron. She became a prophetess and died at Kadesh during the Wilderness wanderings.

mite A coin worth about one-eighth of a cent. Jesus praised the widow who gave two mites, saying that she had given more than the rich because "they did cast in of their abundance; but she of her want cast in all that she had, even all her living."

Mizpah (mĭz′pȧ) and **Mispeh** (mĭz′-pȧ) 1. Jacob and Laban named the heap of rocks which they raised as a witness of their covenant, Galeed and Mizpah.

2. Mizpah is also the name of

several towns and places mentioned in the Old Testament.

Moab (mō′ăb) The son of Lot's eldest daughter. He was the founder of the Moabites, who dwelt in the desert lands at the southeast end of the Dead Sea.

Molech (mō′lĕk) A fire-god to whom human sacrifices were made. He was worshiped by the native Canaanites. The religious leaders of Israel were constantly forced to fight against the adoption of his worship by their people.

Molten (mōl′tɑn) **Sea** or **Brazen** (brā′zn) **Sea** A very large brass basin standing upon 12 sculptured oxen, which Solomon had

made for the Temple. It is said to have measured 15 feet in diameter and 7½ feet in depth and to have held 16,000 to 27,000 gallons of water. The priests used this water for washing their hands and feet before sacrifices.

moneychangers (mŭn′ĭ-chānj-ẽrz) Jews came from many foreign lands to worship in the Temple in Jerusalem. Since only Hebrew coins were acceptable in the Temple, there were moneychangers in the Temple Court to provide the acceptable currency. These men were often dishonest; because of this Jesus overturned their tables.

Mordecai (môr′dĭ-kī) The man whom God chose as an indirect

Jesus Casting Moneychangers from the Temple

deliverer of the Jews from the evil plot of Ahasuerus' (Xerxes') minister of state. Mordecai was Esther's foster father.

Moreh (mō'rĕ) 1. The plain of Moreh was the first stopping place of Abraham and his people after their entrance into Canaan.

2. The hill of Moreh was the place where the Midianites and the Amalekites camped just before Gideon launched his attack against them.

Moriah (mō-rī'ȧ) 1. The place where Abraham prepared to sacrifice his son Isaac to God.

2. The hill where the angel of the Lord appeared to David "by the threshingfloor of Ornan." David bought this sacred place and erected an altar upon it. Many years later his son, King Solomon, built the first Temple on this site. It is the eastern heights of modern Jerusalem.

Moses (mō'zȧz) A great Hebrew prophet and leader. He was in a sense the founder of the Hebrew religion and is known today as one of the greatest lawgivers of the world. He received the tablets with the Ten Commandments from God on Mount Sinai. After leading the Israelites out of bondage in Egypt and through the long years of the Wilderness wanderings, Moses died on Mount Nebo, east of the Jordan and in

Moses

full sight of Canaan, the Promised Land.

Myra (mī'rȧ) A Mediterranean seaport of southwest Asia Minor. There Paul and his centurion guard, on the way to Rome, boarded the ship which was later wrecked.

myrrh (mẽr) A fragrant resin and oil imported into Palestine from Arabia. It was one of the ingredients of "holy anointing oil" and was also used as a perfume, as a medicine, and as an embalming agent. One of the Wise Men brought myrrh as a gift for the infant Jesus.

myrtle (mẽr'tl) A shrub or low tree with shiny green leaves and very fragrant white flowers.

Myrtle

Naaman (nā'a-man)   A famous Syrian general who was cured of leprosy by the Prophet Elisha.

Nabal (nā'bal)   A wealthy sheep owner of Carmel who refused to pay tribute to King David.

Naboth (nā'bŏth)   A man of Jezreel who was falsely accused and stoned to death as the result of the evil scheming of Jezebel. She did this so that her husband, King Ahab, might take possession of Naboth's vineyard.

Nadab (nā'dăb)   1. The eldest son of Aaron and Elisheba. He was one of those chosen from the multitude to worship "afar off" while Moses communed with God on Mount Sinai. Nadab was later struck dead by God because he had not lighted the incense in his censer from the fire which burned perpetually on the altar. He had used ordinary fire instead.

2. King Jeroboam's son. He reigned only two years before being slain by Baasha. In this way were God's warnings fulfilled against Jeroboam and his house.

Nahash (nā'hăsh)   The king of the Ammonites who demanded of all the people of Jabesh-gilead the loss of their right eyes or slavery. Infuriated by this cruel dictate, King Saul led an army against the Ammonites and defeated them.

Nahor (nā'hôr)   1. The grandfather of Abraham.

2. The brother of Abraham and Haran.

Nahum (nā'hŭm)   A minor Hebrew prophet and author of an Old Testament book. The Book of Nahum contains his prophecies against Nineveh.

Nain (nā'ĭn)   The village in Galilee where Jesus raised a widow's son from the dead.

Naioth (nā'ŏth)   The place where David went with Samuel seeking refuge from the fury of his father-in-law, King Saul.

Naomi (nā-ō'mĭ)   The wife of Elimelech and the mother of Chilion and Mahlon. She became the mother-in-law of Orpah and Ruth. After the tragic deaths of her husband and sons she left Moab and returned to her home in Bethlehem, taking Ruth with her.

Naphtali (năf'ta-lī)   Jacob's son by Bilhah, Rachel's maidservant. He was the founder of one of the Twelve Tribes of Israel.

Nathan (nā'than)   A distinguished

prophet who lived during the reigns of David and Solomon.

Nathanael (na-thăn'ā-ĕl) One of the Twelve Apostles. He was a native of Cana in Galilee and was brought to Jesus by Philip. He is known as Bartholomew in the first three Gospels.

Nazarene (năz-a-rēn') An inhabitant of Nazareth. Jesus is often called a Nazarene.

Nazareth (năz'a-rĕth) A very ancient village in Galilee, where Jesus spent his boyhood and early manhood.

Nazarite (năz'a-rīt), more properly **Nazirite** (năz'ĭ-rīt) A person who took certain vows and devoted himself to God, either for a particular period of time or for life. Samson was a Nazirite. Samuel, John the Baptist, Anna the prophetess and Paul may also have taken these vows.

Nebaioth (nĭ-bā'yŏth) or **Nebajoth** (nĭ-bā'jŏth) The first-born son of Ishmael and grandson of Hagar and Abraham. He was the founder of an Arabian tribe.

Nebo (nē'bō), **Mount** The mountain just east of the Jordan at the northern end of the Dead Sea, from which Moses first saw the land of Canaan, the land which God had promised to the Children of Israel. Moses died there.

Nebuchadnezzar (nĕb-ū-kad-nĕz'-ĕr) A great and powerful king of Babylon who ruled for about 40 years. He invaded the land of Israel several times, carrying the people into bondage in Babylon. In the end he razed Jerusalem and the holy Temple, so that for more than a hundred years it remained what Isaiah called a wilderness of "thorns and briers." The Old Testament books of Lamentations, Isaiah and Jeremiah, and the Second Book of Kings deal in whole or in part with this period.

Nebuzar-adan (nĕb-ū-zär=ā'dăn) The captain of Nebuchadnezzar's bodyguard. He directed the destruction of the Temple and the walls of Jerusalem.

Necho (nē'kō) An Egyptian king who invaded Palestine and treacherously killed King Josiah at a "friendly" meeting at Megiddo. Necho then held the Kingdom of Judah as a vassal state. He finally lost this territory to Nebuchadnezzar.

Neginah

neginah (nĕ-gē′nä) The general term used to describe all stringed instruments. This word appears in the title of several psalms. The plural is neginoth.

Nehemiah (nē-hĭ-mī′à) A man of the Tribe of Judah who gained great favor at the Persian court and served as cupbearer to the king. However, learning of Jerusalem's plight as a result of Nebuchadnezzar's destruction over a hundred years before, he went to Jerusalem with the Persian king's permission and rebuilt the walls of the city and started the restoration of the Temple. An account of his life and work is contained in the Old Testament book which bears his name.

Nehushtan (nĭ-hŭsh′tàn) The name meaning "thing of brass" given by King Hezekiah to the bronze serpent which Moses had made in the Wilderness. King Hezekiah destroyed this serpent during his religious reforms.

Nethinims (nĕth′ĭ-nĭmz) Temple servants who performed unimportant religious tasks, thus freeing the Levites, or priestly class, for the more important Temple duties.

New Testament The second portion of the Bible. It contains accounts of the life and teachings of Jesus and accounts of the Early Christian Church and its theology. The word "testament" means "covenant" or "solemn agreement." The New Testament means "the new covenant between God and man" as contrasted with the Old Testament, or "old covenant between God and man." There are 27 books in the New Testament.

Nicodemus (nĭk-ō-dē′màs) A Pharisee and member of the Sanhedrin, who sought out Jesus at night to learn about His teachings. He spoke in defense of Jesus during one of His trials. After the Crucifixion he and Joseph of Arimathaea took Jesus from the cross and buried Him in the new tomb in Joseph's garden.

Nicolas (nĭk′ō-làs) A native of Antioch who became a Christian and who was chosen as one of the first seven deacons of the Early Church in Jerusalem.

Nimrim (nĭm′rĭm), **the waters of** A stream in Moab mentioned by Isaiah and Jeremiah.

Nimrod (nĭm′rŏd) A son of Cush and a grandson of Noah. He was a "mighty hunter" and founder of kingdoms.

Nineveh (nĭn′à-vĕ) The capital of ancient Assyria. It is said to have been founded by Nimrod. Nahum and Zephaniah prophesied against Nineveh, and Jonah preached repentance to its people in obedience to God's wishes.

Noah (nō′a) Son of Lamech, grandson of Methuselah and tenth in direct line from Adam. He was a "just man" and "found grace in the eyes of the Lord." Because of this God commanded him to build an ark to save himself, his family and the animals from the Flood.

Nob (nōb) A town near Jerusalem that belonged to priests who were friendly to David. King Saul ordered that these priests be killed. Doeg, the Edomite, who executed this dreadful deed, carried this order still further and massacred all the inhabitants of Nob as well as all the livestock.

Nod (nŏd) The land to which Cain fled after murdering his brother Abel.

Numbers (nŭm′bĕrz) The fourth book of the Pentateuch. It contains the story of the Wilderness wanderings from the time the Israelites left Sinai to the time they entered Canaan 38 years later. It takes its name from the two "numberings" of the people of Israel, or the double census which it describes.

Nun (nŭn) The father of Joshua.

Obadiah (ō-ba-dī′a) 1. A minor prophet who wrote the shortest book of the Old Testament. It is a denunciation of the Edomites.
2. An officer of rank in King Ahab's court. He was a devout believer in God. During the persecution by the evil queen, Jezebel, he hid, at the risk of his life, over 100 prophets.

Obed (ō′bĕd) The son of Ruth and Boaz. He became the father of Jesse and, through him, the grandfather of King David.

Obed–edom (ō-bĕd=ē′dam) A Levite of the city of Gath or of Gathrimmon. The Ark of the Covenant rested in his house for 3 months before King David took it to Jerusalem.

Oded (ō′dĕd) 1. The father of the Prophet Azariah.
2. A prophet in Israel during the reign of Pekah. He persuaded the army of the Northern Kingdom to treat the captives from Judah with kindness and to return them to their own land.

Og

Og (ŏg) A giant who was once king of Bashan, a land just east of the Jordan. He ruled over 60 cities. He and his people were defeated and exterminated by the Israelites shortly before they entered Canaan.

Old Testament (tĕs'tà-mànt) "Testament" means "covenant" or "agreement." The Old Testament is the first part of the Bible, or the "old covenant between God and man" as compared to the New Testament or "the new covenant between God and man." There are 39 books in the Old Testament.

Olives (ŏl'ĭvz), **Mount of** A hill or mount east of Jerusalem, close to the city wall. It was the scene of many stirring events of both the Old and New Testaments. Jesus and His disciples often spent the night on the Mount of Olives. It was there, in the Garden of Gethsemane, that He was betrayed by Judas and arrested by the Romans.

Omega

Omega (ō-mē'gà) The last letter of the Greek alphabet. It is used as a figure of speech to denote the end of anything.

Omri (ŏm'rī) A commander of the army of the Northern Kingdom who was chosen by the people as their king. He founded a dynasty;

his son Ahab succeeded him to the throne. Omri proved to be an evil ruler.

Onan (ō'năn) A son of Judah and a grandson of Jacob. He did evil in the sight of God, so God slew him as He had also slain his evil elder brother, Er.

Onesimus (ō-nĕs'ĭ-màs) A slave living in Colosse, a city in Asia Minor. He escaped from his Christian master, Philemon, and went to Rome, where he became a Christian and an intimate friend of Paul. Paul insisted that Onesimus return to his master and wrote a letter to Philemon in his behalf. The Epistle to Philemon is part of the New Testament.

Onesiphorus (ŏn-ĭ-sĭf'ō-rŭs) A man of Ephesus, a city in Asia Minor. Paul writes of him with deep gratitude. He says that Onesiphorus proved a true friend to him when he was a prisoner in Rome.

Ophel (ō'fĕl) A hill south of the Temple mount. It was part of ancient Jerusalem. The Pool of Siloam was at its base.

Ophir (ō'fēr) A place from which the Hebrews obtained exceptionally fine gold in Solomon's time. It is not known whether this place was in India, Arabia or Africa.

Ophrah (ŏf'rà) A town or place, probably near Shechem, which was the home of Gideon. It was there that he fought the worship of the pagan god, Baal, and there that he was buried.

Oreb (ō'rĕb) One of two Midianite brothers slain at Gideon's command. The name Oreb means "raven."

Orpah (ôr'pä) The Moabite woman who married Naomi's son Chilion. When Chilion died, Orpah stayed in Moab with her own people instead of going to Bethlehem with Naomi, as Ruth did.

Othniel (ŏth'nĭ-ĕl) Caleb's younger brother. He became the first judge in Israel after Joshua.

Ozem (ō'zĕm) The sixth son of Jesse and one of David's brothers.

P

Padan–aram (pā-dăn=a'răm) The section of Mesopotamia to which Abraham sent his servants in search of a wife for his son Isaac. Jacob's wives also came from this district.

Palestine (păl'ĕs-tīn) The name used in Roman times for the lands, both east and west of the Jordan, inhabited by the people of Israel. This term has survived to the present day.

Pamphylia (păm-fĭl'ĭ-á) A Roman coastal province of Asia Minor. Paul and Barnabas went as missionaries to this land.

Paphos (pā'fŏs) A town at the west end of Cyprus visited by Paul and Barnabas.

parable (păr'á-bl) An utterance or short narrative which illustrates a truth or moral lesson. Jesus used many parables to illustrate the truths of His teachings.

Paradise (păr'á-dīs) A word of Persian origin which means "an orchard of pleasure and fruits" or "a garden." The Garden of Eden is often referred to as Paradise. Heaven is also sometimes called paradise.

Paran (pā'rán) The wilderness in the east-central section of the Sinai Peninsula to which Ishmael and his mother, Hagar, fled when they were banished from Abraham's tribe. Centuries later the Israelites wandered for many years through this same desolate region while going from Egypt to Canaan.

Parmenas (pär'mĭ-năs) One of the 7 deacons mentioned in The Acts as being "men of honest report, full of the Holy Ghost and wisdom."

Parthians (pär'thĭ-ănz) The name used in The Acts to designate certain Jews who were among those gathered together with the Apostles in Jerusalem on the Day of Pentecost. The Parthians came from Parthia, a mountainous district south of the Caspian Sea.

Pashur (păsh'ẽr) 1. A man in the reign of Jehoiakim who put the Prophet Jeremiah in stocks near one of the gates of Jerusalem for prophesying that all sorts of horrors would befall the people. He felt that Jeremiah was undermining public morale.

2. A member of a priestly family who with others petitioned King Zedekiah to slay Jeremiah as a traitor for speaking in favor of the Babylonians, who under Nebuchadnezzar were about to attack Jerusalem.

Passover (păs'ō-vẽr) The first of three great yearly festivals of the Jews. It takes place in the spring of the year and is held in commemoration of the time when God led the Jews out of bondage in Egypt. The word "Passover" refers to the fact that the destroying angel "passed over" the homes of the Jews when he slew the firstborn males of man and beast in Egypt.

Patmos (păt'mŏs) A small rocky island in the Aegean Sea off the coast of Asia Minor. There the Apostle John saw a vision and heard the great voice saying, "I am Alpha and Omega, the first and the last."

patriarch (pā'trĭ-ärk) The title used in Old Testament times to designate the head of a family or tribe. It is used especially in re-

Patriarch

ferring to those, such as Abraham, Isaac and Jacob, who lived before the time of Moses.

Paul (pôl) The name of the first Christian missionary. Paul was a Jew from Tarsus and took a very active part in the persecution of the early Christians in Jerusalem. Following a vision on the road to

Paul

Damascus, he became a believer in Jesus. Ever after, he was a fervent Christian and spent his life spreading the Gospel in Greece, Rome and Asia Minor. His epistles, or letters, are included in the New Testament. Parts of his life are told in The Acts. He was beheaded in Rome at Nero's command.

Pekah (pē'kä) An army officer who murdered the reigning king of the Northern Kingdom and seized the throne.

Pentateuch (pĕn'tȧ-tūk) The first five books of the Old Testament. The Hebrews, or Jews, call these five books the Torah, meaning "the Law."

Pentecost (pĕn'tĭ-kŏst) Pentecost, meaning "fiftieth day," is another name for the Hebrew Feast of Weeks, Feast of Harvest, or Day of Weeks. This is a thanksgiving celebration, and it always occurs on the fiftieth day after Passover. In the Christian Church, Pentecost is the day of memorial of the coming of the Holy Spirit to the disciples at Jerusalem after the Ascension of Christ.

Peor (pē'ôr) A mountain peak in Moab to which the Mesopotamian prophet Balaam was taken by Balak, king of Moab, so that he might look down upon the wandering Israelites and curse them.

Pergamos (pẽr'gȧ-mŏs) A city in Asia Minor which the Apostle John called "Satan's seat." One of the "seven churches of Asia" was there.

Persia (pẽr'zhȧ) The name applied to a vast country or empire extending at various times from India to the Black Sea and the Mediterranean.

Peter (pē'tẽr) The name meaning "rock" which Jesus gave to the disciple Simon, brother of Andrew. These brothers were fishermen at the Sea of Galilee. It was to them that Jesus said, "Follow me, and I will make you fishers of men." Two books of the New Testament are attributed to Peter.

Phanuel (fȧ-nū'ĕl) The father of Anna the Prophetess. He was of the Tribe of Aser.

Pharaoh

Pharaoh (fār'ō) The common title of the kings of Egypt. It means "great house," and was used as a term of reverence.

Pharisees (făr'ĭ-sēz) An ancient religious sect of the Jews. These people were extremely devout and strict in their adherence to religious laws. Jesus criticized them because He said that they weighed down the people with rituals and laws. He also accused them of being hypocrites. The Pharisees criticized Jesus because they felt He was breaking down their religious laws. They felt that He was committing heresy.

Phenice (fĭ-nī'sĭ) or **Phoenicia** (fĭ-nĭsh'ĭ-à) An ancient country on the Mediterranean north of Palestine. Tyre and Sidon were its chief cities.

Philadelphia (fĭl-à-dĕl'fĭ-à) An ancient city in Asia Minor. One of the "seven churches of Asia" was located there.

Philemon (fĭ-lē'màn) The master in Colosse to whom Paul addressed his epistle about the slave Onesimus.

Philip (fĭl'ĭp) A man from Bethsaida of Galilee who became one of the Twelve Apostles. He brought Bartholomew, also known as Nathanael, to Jesus. Bartholomew also became an apostle.

Philip (fĭl'ĭp) **the Evangelist** (ĭ-văn'jà-lĭst) One of the 7 deacons of the Early Church in Jerusalem. It was his duty to distribute food and alms among the disciples.

He later preached the Gospel in Palestine. Paul was his friend.

Philippi (fĭ-lĭp'ī) A city of Macedonia. It was in Philippi that the Gospel was first preached in Europe. Lydia, a woman of Philippi, became the first Christian convert of Europe. Paul visited Philippi several times. It was there that he and Silas were imprisoned on false charges.

Philippians (fĭ-lĭp'ĭ-ànz), **Epistle to the** A letter written by Paul while he was imprisoned in Rome, to the church at Philippi in Macedonia.

Philistines (fĭ-lĭs'tĭnz) A people who lived in a fertile plain bordering on the Mediterranean in the southwestern part of Palestine. Their country was called Philistia.

Phinehas (fĭn'ĭ-às) 1. The son of Eleazar and grandson of Aaron. He became High Priest and is famous for the fight he waged against those pagan beliefs of the people of Moab which had been adopted by the Israelites.

2. The younger son of Eli, the priest at Shiloh. He and his brother were killed in battle on the day when the Ark of the Covenant was captured by the Philistines.

Phrygia (frĭj'ĭ-à) A large district in Asia Minor visited by Paul during his Second and Third Missionary Journeys.

Jesus Before Pontius Pilate

phylactery (fĭ-lăk′tẽr-ĭ) A small leather case containing strips of parchment inscribed with passages from the Pentateuch. Phylacteries are attached to long leather strips and are worn on the forehead or on the bend of the left arm, with the leather thong wound about the forearm. They are used by the Jewish people during periods of prayer.

Phylactery

Pilate (pī′lȧt), **Pontius** (pŏn′shȧs) The fifth Roman procurator or military governor of Judaea. Jesus was tried by Pontius Pilate and crucified at his orders.

Pisgah (pĭz′gȧ) A mountain range just east of the Jordan. Its highest peak is Mount Nebo, the place where Moses died.

Pisidia (pĭ-sĭd′ĭ-ȧ) A district in southern Asia Minor. Paul and Barnabas visited there on the First Missionary Journey.

Pontus (pŏn′tȧs) A large district in Asia Minor bordering on the Black Sea.

Potiphar (pŏt′ĭ-fẽr) The Egyptian

captain of Pharaoh's guard who bought Joseph as a slave. Potiphar's wife falsely accused Joseph and because of this Potiphar put him in prison.

Potipherah (pō-tĭf'ĕr-à) An Egyptian priest and the father of Asenath, Joseph's wife.

Priscilla (prĭ-sĭl'à) The wife of Aquila. She and her husband worked with Paul and became Christians.

Prochorus (prŏk'ō-ràs) One of the 7 deacons of the Early Church in Jerusalem. He was next after Stephen and Philip.

Proconsul

proconsul (prō-kŏn'sàl) A Roman civil administrator of a peaceful province.

procurator (prŏk'ū-rā-tẽr) The Roman military governor of a rebellious province.

prodigal Squandering of wealth or indulging in reckless extravagance. One of the most famous parables spoken by Jesus was the Parable of the Prodigal Son.

prophet (prŏf'ĕt) A Biblical prophet was one inspired by God to speak in His name, revealing the future in regard to both material and spiritual matters.

Proverbs (prŏv'ĕrbz), **The** A book of the Old Testament. It contains the sayings of wise men of Israel, including Solomon.

Psalms (sämz), **The Book of** A book of the Old Testament containing 150 religious poems. These were designed to be set to music and used in the worship of God in the Temple. They are used today by both Christians and Jews.

psaltery (sôl'tẽr-ĭ) A stringed musical instrument used for accompanying the voice in song.

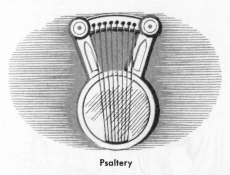

Psaltery

Ptolemy (tŏl'ĭ-mĭ) The common name of the Greek dynasty of Egyptian kings. This royal house was founded by a Macedonian of low rank after Alexander the Great had conquered Egypt and after he had died.

publican (pŭb'lĭ-k*a*n) A tax collector for the Roman conqueror. Publicans were greatly disliked by the Jews of Jesus' day.

Publius (pŭb'lĭ-*a*s) A friendly man of the island of Melita who received Paul and his companions into his home following the shipwreck. He may have been the governor of the island.

Purim (pū'rĭm) The annual Hebrew festival commemorating the escape of the Jews from a persecution planned by Haman, the minister of state to Ahasuerus (Xerxes), the king of Persia. It was instituted by Mordecai, Esther's foster father.

Q

Quartus (kwôr'tǎs) A Christian known to Paul. He is mentioned in the Epistle to the Romans.

queen of heaven The pagan goddess Ishtar of Babylon. The Prophet Jeremiah denounced her worship as displeasing to God.

R

Rabbah (răb'*a*) or **Rabbath** (răb'-*a*th) A fortified city east of the Jordan which belonged to the Ammonites. It was there that the giant, King Og of Bashan, was buried. The name of Rabbah was changed to Philadelphia

in honor of the Egyptian king Philadelphus.

Rabbi (răb'ī) A title of respect, meaning master or teacher, given by the Jews to their spiritual leaders. Jesus was often called Rabbi.

raca (r*a*-kä') An Aramaic word of contempt meaning "empty" or "worthless."

Rachel (rā'ch*a*l) The daughter of Laban and the sister of Leah. She was greatly loved by her husband, Jacob, and was the mother of his sons, Joseph and Benjamin. She was buried near Bethlehem.

Rahab (rā'hăb) A woman of Jericho who helped Joshua's spies. Because of this, Rahab and her family were led safely out of the city when Joshua's forces besieged it and burned it to the ground.

Ramah (rā'm*a*) The name of several towns and places mentioned in the Old Testament. It was near Ramah of Benjamin that Deborah, the prophetess, sat beneath a palm tree and judged Israel. It was in Ramah of Ephraim that Samuel was born to Hannah and Elkanah.

Rameses (răm'ĭ-sēz) 1. The name of eleven Pharaohs of Egypt. The Pharaoh of the Exodus was Rameses II.

2. A city and district in the

land of Goshen in lower Egypt where the Israelites settled.

3. The name of one of the two store cities built for the Pharaoh. The other was called Pithom. It was from Rameses that the Israelites started the Exodus.

Ramoth–gilead (rā-mŏth=gĭl'ĭ-ad) An ancient city of Gilead, a district east of the Jordan and south of the Sea of Galilee. Ramoth-gilead was the scene of many Old Testament events.

Rebekah (rĭ-bĕk'a) The beautiful daughter of Bethuel and sister of Laban. Abraham's servants brought her back from Mesopotamia as a wife for his son Isaac. She became the mother of Esau and Jacob.

Rechab (rē'kăb) One of the two "captains of the guard" who murdered King Ishbosheth, Saul's youngest son.

Rehoboam (rē-hō-bō'ăm) Solomon's son by the Ammonite princess, Naamah. He succeeded his father to the throne, but because of his arrogance the Northern Tribes of Israel revolted and set up a kingdom of their own. Only the Tribes of Judah and Benjamin remained faithful to him. Thus the land of Israel was divided into two kingdoms—Northern Kingdom or the Kingdom of Israel and the Southern Kingdom or the Kingdom of Judah.

Rephaim (rĕf'ā-ĭm), **Valley of** The "valley of the giants" near Jerusalem. It was there that David defeated the Philistines in two separate battles.

Rephidim (rĕf'ĭ-dĭm) A campsite of the Children of Israel as they neared Mount Sinai. It was there that Moses struck a rock and

Moses at Rephidim

brought forth water when his people complained because of their thirst. Rephidim is also remembered as the place where the Israelites under Joshua defeated the Amalekites in battle while Aaron and Hur supported Moses' uplifted hands.

Resurrection (rĕz-a-rĕk'shan) The rising again from the dead. Belief in the resurrection is an important part of the Christian faith and was fully exemplified through the Resurrection of Jesus.

Reuben (rōō'běn) Jacob's first-born child. Leah was his mother. Reuben seems to have been a good man, but his father did not admire him too much. He referred to him as being "unstable as water." Reuben was the founder of one of the Twelve Tribes of Israel.

Revelation (rĕv-a-lā'shan) The last book of the New Testament, sometimes referred to as the Apocalypse, the Greek word for "revelation." It is made up of a series of prophetic visions and is attributed to the Apostle John.

Rhoda (rō'da) The young girl who announced to those gathered in the home of Mary, the mother of Mark, that Peter was knocking at the door. This incident occurred following his miraculous escape from Herod's prison.

Rhodes (rōdz) The name of a famous Greek city and island lying between the coast of Asia Minor and Crete. Paul visited there during his Third Missionary Journey.

Riblah (rĭb'la) A very ancient town on the road between Babylon and Palestine. Nebuchadnezzar waited there while his

Colossus of Rhodes

armies besieged Jerusalem and Tyre. The Egyptian Pharaoh, Necho, also waited in Riblah for King Jehoahaz of Judah to come to him from Jerusalem. There he put him in chains before taking him to Egypt as a prisoner. In Riblah King Zedekiah of Judah was blinded, at Nebuchadnezzar's command, after having witnessed the slaying of his sons.

Rizpah (rĭz'pä) The mother of 2 of the 7 sons of Saul who were hanged by the Gibeonites.

Romans (rō'manz), **Epistle to the** A letter written by Paul from Corinth to the young church in Rome. It is a New Testament book and is considered one of Paul's most important epistles.

Rufus (rōō'fas) One of the two sons of Simon of Cyrene, the man who carried the cross for Jesus.

The other son was named Alexander. All three joined the very earliest Christian group in Jerusalem following the Crucifixion.

Ruth (rōōth) A young woman of Moab who married Naomi's son Mahlon. When he died she went to Bethlehem with Naomi. There she married Boaz and gave birth to a son, Obed. Through his line she became the great-grandmother of King David. Her story is told in the Old Testament Book of Ruth.

Sabaoth (săb'ā-ŏth) A Hebrew word meaning "armies" or "hosts." Jehovah Sabaoth means Lord of hosts.

Sabbath (săb'áth) The name meaning "a day of rest," which the Jewish people apply to the seventh and last day of the week. According to Genesis, God instituted this day of rest for man and beast. The Christian Church observes the Sabbath on the first day of the week, or the Lord's Day. The Seventh Day Adventists observe the seventh day.

Sabbatical (sá-băt'ĭ-kál) **Year** According to the Mosaic Law every seventh year was to be kept holy. For 6 years the people were allowed to sow and reap and cultivate their vineyards, but during the seventh year the land must lie at rest, "that the poor of thy people may eat: and what they leave the beasts of the field shall eat." It was also decreed that all debts should be forgiven during the seventh year.

sackcloth (săk'clôth) A coarse dark cloth made of goat's hair. It was used for making sacks and for the rough garments of mourners. These were sometimes worn next to the skin.

sacrifice (săk'rĭ-fīs) An offering to God as prescribed by ancient ritual. Peace offerings and thank offerings were placed on the altar of God. Animals were sacrificed to atone for sin. The first fruits of the crop were given to the Lord as a thank offering.

Sadducees (săd'ū-sēz) A religious division, or school of Jews, at the time of Jesus. They were in opposition to the Pharisees and did not believe in resurrection, immortality, or reward and punishment after death. Neither did they believe in spirits and angels. They believed strongly in personal freedom of will. The Sadducees comprised only a small group but were very wealthy and influential. The higher priests belonged to this group.

Salamis (săl'á-mĭs) A city at the east end of the island of Cyprus. It was visited by Paul and Barnabas on the First Missionary Journey.

Salem (sā'lĕm) The place of which

Sacrifice

King Melchizedek was ruler. It is believed that in early times Salem was another name for Jerusalem.

Salmon (săl'mἀn) or **Salma** (săl'mἀ) The father of Boaz, Ruth's second husband.

Salome (sἀ-lō'mĭ) 1. The wife of Zebedee and the mother of the Apostles James and John. She is believed by many to have been the sister of Mary, the mother of Jesus. She and Mary Magdalene and Mary, the mother of James, found Jesus' tomb empty on the Resurrection morning.

2. The daughter of Herodias, wife of Herod Antipas. Under the influence of her evil mother, Salome asked for the head of John the Baptist.

Salt Sea The most ancient name for the Dead Sea. It is first mentioned in Genesis.

Salt Sea

Samaria (sἀ-mâr'ĭ-ἀ) 1. A city in the central part of Palestine. It was built by King Omri as the capital of the Northern Kingdom.

2. At the time of Jesus, Samaria was not only the name of Omri's city, but also the name of the middle district of Palestine.

Samaritans (sἀ-măr'ĭ-tἀnz) In the

days of the divided kingdoms of Israel and Judah, all the Jews of the Northern Kingdom were known as Samaritans. However, in the time of Jesus the Samaritans were quite another people. Following the captivity of the people of Israel by the Assyrians, the city of Samaria and the surrounding district were depopulated of all Jews, and Babylonians were settled in this area. Through the centuries that followed, these people adopted many of the religious beliefs of the Jews but at the same time they retained many of their Gentile beliefs. Because of this they were never accepted by the Jews and an animosity existed between them.

Samson (săm's'n) A judge of Israel and the strongest man mentioned in the Bible. He was born near Jerusalem and before birth was consecrated to God as a Nazirite. An angel announced that he would begin to deliver Israel from

Samson

the Philistines. Samson lived according to his Nazirite vows, which prohibited the cutting of his hair. His strength depended on this. In fulfilment of the angel's words he killed many Philistines. He died in the temple of Dagon at Gaza after having been betrayed by Delilah and brutally blinded by the Philistines.

Hannah Presenting Samuel

Samuel (săm'ū-ăl) The son of Hannah and Elkanah and a prophet and judge of Israel. He was dedicated before birth to the service of God and brought up by the old priest Eli at Shiloh. He established several schools for the training and education of young men, and delivered the Israelites at Mizpah from the oppression of the Philistines. He anointed Saul as the first king of Israel in response to the demands of the people.

Samuel (săm'ū-ăl), **First and Second Books of** Two books of the Old Testament which give the history of Israel from the birth of Samuel to the old age of King David.

Sanballat (săn-băl′at) An official in Samaria at the time Nehemiah began to rebuild the walls of Jerusalem. He did all he could to obstruct Nehemiah's work.

Sanhedrin (săn′hĭ-drĭn) The supreme council of seventy which governed and judged the religious and civil life of the Jews. Its members seem to have been priests, elders, men of age and experience, scribes and lawyers. This council had once exercised the power of life and death, but in Jesus' time it no longer held this power. Jesus was tried before the Sanhedrin.

Sapphira (să-fī′ra) The wife of Ananias. Both she and her husband, members of the Early Christian Church, fell dead because they had lied to God.

Sarah (sâr′a) or **Sara** (sâr′a) Abraham's wife and the mother of Isaac. She was buried in the cave at Machpelah.

Sardis (sär′dĭs) The capital of Lydia in Asia Minor. It is mentioned in Revelation.

Sargon (sär′gŏn) A great and powerful Assyrian king. After he ascended the throne the city of Samaria and the surrounding countryside were captured by the Assyrians.

Satan (sā′tan) A Hebrew word meaning adversary or enemy. In the Bible the word Satan refers to an evil power which is at work in the world and which stands in opposition to God. In a more personal sense it refers to the chief of all the evil spirits. Satan is referred to in the Bible by many other names, such as: the Devil, the Tempter, Beelzebub, the serpent, and the dragon.

Saul (sôl) The first king of Israel; anointed by the Prophet Samuel. He spent his life fighting the Philistines and died with three of his sons at the battle of Gilboa. He had suffered presentiments of doom and before the battle had consulted the "witch of En-dor." Saul had an unstable temperament and was subject to intense jealousy. His love for young David was constantly overshadowed by this weakness.

saviour (sāv′yẽr) One who saves or redeems. In the New Testament this term applies specifically to Jesus.

Scapegoat

scapegoat (skāp'gōt) A goat upon which the High Priest symbolically loaded the sins of the people on the Day of Atonement. The goat was then driven out into the wilderness, thus carrying away the sins.

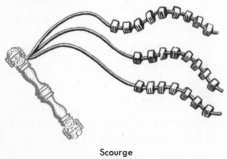

Scourge

scourge (skĕrj) A short whip usually made of 3 leather thongs, either knotted or with pieces of metal attached for bruising and tearing the flesh.

scribes These men were scholars and interpreters of the Mosaic Law. In New Testament times their decisions constituted a new oral religious law as binding as the written Mosaic Law. The Pharisees accepted this oral law; the Sadducees rejected it.

Scrip

scrip A bag, usually of leather, in which the shepherds and farmers of Palestine carried their food and other necessary articles.

Scripture (skrĭp'tẽr) A general term meaning "writing" which is applied to all the material contained in the Bible. In New Testament times, the term Scripture or Scriptures referred only to the sacred books of the people of Israel.

Scythian (sĭth'ĭ-an) The name used in the Bible to denote all the tribes which lived north of the Black and Caspian Seas. These people were considered very low and primitive and the term meant ignorant, rude or degraded.

Secundus (sĭ-kŭn'dăs) A Christian from the city of Thessalonica in Macedonia who went with Paul into Asia Minor.

Seir (sē'ĭr) A mountain range and land lying south of the Dead Sea. It is referred to in Genesis. This land was later inhabited by the descendants of Esau and became known as the land of Edom.

Selah (sē'la) A word which appears 71 times in The Psalms and three times in Habakkuk. Its meaning is unknown, but it is believed to have been an exclamation such as "amen" or "hallelujah" which was used by the worshipers or priests at specified moments in the service.

Seleucia (sĭ-lū'shĭ-*a*) A strong fortress and seaport on the Syrian coast. Paul and Barnabas set sail from there on the First Missionary Journey.

Senir (sē'nĭr) or **Shenir** (shē'nĕr) The Amorite name for Mount Hermon.

Sennacherib (s*a*-năk'ĕr-ĭb) A powerful Assyrian king who invaded Palestine about 701 B.C. However, a miraculous event occurred. In answer to the prayers of King Hezekiah of Judah, God destroyed most of the invading army, and Sennacherib fled back to his own country. He was later murdered by two of his sons.

sepulcher (sĕp'*a*l-kĕr) A tomb or burial place such as a cave. These were carefully whitened once a year. Thus it was that Jesus compared the hypocritical Pharisees to "whited sepulchres" which are beautiful on the outside but are unclean within.

Seraiah (sĭ-rā'y*a*) "A quiet prince" of Judah who went with King Zedekiah into Babylon. The Prophet Jeremiah gave this young man a book in which he had written prophecies against Babylon. He told him to read the book and then "bind a stone to it" and throw it into the Euphrates River. "Thus," said Jeremiah, "shall Babylon sink."

Sepulcher

Seraphim

seraphim (sĕr'*a*-fĭm) Celestial beings that Isaiah saw in a vision standing above God's throne. They each had three pairs of wings. They covered their faces in humility with one pair. With another pair they covered their feet in respect. They flew with the third pair. Seraphim acted as messengers between heaven and earth.

Sergius Paulus (sẽr'jĭ-ȧs pô'lȧs) The name of the Roman proconsul of Cyprus when Paul and Barnabas visited that island during the First Missionary Journey. He was a just and intelligent man and readily admitted the truths of the Gospel.

Seth (sĕth) The third son of Adam and Eve. He was born after Cain murdered Abel.

Shadrach (shā'drăk) The Chaldean name given to one of Daniel's three companions who miraculously survived the fiery furnace. The other two were called Abednego and Meshach.

Shallum (shăl'ȧm) A man who plotted against and killed King Zechariah, thus bringing the dynasty of Jehu to a close. Shallum then mounted the throne as fifteenth ruler of the Northern Kingdom.

Shalmaneser (shăl-man-ē'zẽr) The Assyrian king who invaded the Kingdom of Israel during the reign of Hoshea.

Shamgar (shăm'gär) A deliverer of Israel. He killed 600 Philistines with an oxgoad, a metal-tipped pole used for driving oxen.

Shaphan (shā'fȧn) Secretary or scribe to King Josiah. Hilkiah, the priest, gave Shaphan the newly found Book of the Law, or Deuteronomy, to read. Shaphan helped in carrying out the religious reforms which resulted from this discovery.

Sharon (shăr'ȧn) 1. A beautiful fertile plain between Mount Carmel and the Mediterranean.

2. An unidentified district east of the Jordan near Gilead and Bashan.

shearing house A place on the road between Jezreel and Samaria where King Jehu of the Northern Kingdom met and murdered 42 members of the royal house of Judah.

Sheba (shē'bȧ) The man who led an insurrection against King David directly after the conclusion of Absalom's revolt. He hoped to gain control of northern Israel but was pursued by Joab and finally beheaded.

Sheba (shē'bȧ), **Queen of** The queen of a land in southwestern Arabia. She went to visit and question King Solomon, taking with her a great train of camels. They were laden with many wonderful things, including spices, gold, and precious stones.

Queen of Sheba

Shebah (shē'bȧ) The famous well, also known as Beer-sheba, in southern Palestine which was originally dug by Abraham and later redug by Isaac. Isaac had to do this because his enemies had filled up the well.

Shebna (shĕb'nȧ) A wealthy man who served as secretary or scribe at King Hezekiah's court. He prepared a fine burial place for himself in a cave. For this he was rebuked by the Prophet Isaiah, who predicted that he would never use his sepulcher but would be carried away into captivity instead.

Shechem (shē'kĕm) An ancient city situated in the beautiful valley between Mount Ebal and Mount Gerizim, 32 miles north of Jerusalem. It was there that Abraham pitched his tent and built an altar under the oak of Moreh and there that Jacob bought a "parcel of a field" and dug a well. It was also there that the Israelites heard the curses read from Mount Ebal and the blessings read from Mount Gerizim. In Shechem Joshua delivered his last counsels to the people before his death. It was at Jacob's Well in Shechem that Jesus spoke with the Samaritan woman.

sheep gate One of the gates in the wall of Jerusalem as rebuilt by Nehemiah.

shekel (shĕk'ȧl) In earliest Biblical days this term referred to a standard weight for uncoined metal. About 200 years before Jesus, it came to mean a coin worth about 65 cents. The shekel was in common use during New Testament times.

Shekel

Shem (shĕm) Noah's eldest son and the forefather of all the peoples of Asia Minor, Assyria, and Arabia. The languages spoken by these people and their descendants are known as Shemitic or Semitic languages.

Shemaiah (shĭ-mā'yȧ) A prophet in the reign of Solomon's son and successor, King Rehoboam. He forbade Rehoboam to make war against the northern Tribes of Israel that had revolted and formed the Kingdom of Israel, or the Northern Kingdom.

Shemer (shē′mĕr) The man from whom King Omri bought the hill of Samaria as a site for the capital of the Northern Kingdom.

shewbread (shō′brĕd) or **showbread** Every Sabbath twelve loaves of newly baked unleavened bread, or shewbread, were placed upon a table in the Temple sanc-

Shewbread

tuary or Holy Place next to the seven-branched candlestick and the altar of incense. These twelve loaves represented the Twelve Tribes of Israel. Each Sabbath when the new loaves were brought in, the priests in the sanctuary ate the old loaves, for these could not be removed from the Holy Place.

Shibboleth (shĭb′bō-lĕth) The Israelites west of the Jordan pro-

nounced *sh* as *s*. Thus it was that the people of Gilead used the word "Shibboleth," after their victory over the people of Ephraim, to test who belonged among them and who were enemies. Forty-two thousand Ephraimites were in this way discovered in their midst and killed. Today the word "shibboleth" is used to mean "test word" or "pet phrase."

Shiloh (shī′lō) A sacred town about 20 miles north of Jerusalem. The Tabernacle was located there and the Ark of the Covenant was kept there from the days when the Israelites entered Canaan until it was captured in battle by the Philistines. Eli and Samuel served God at Shiloh.

Shimei (shĭm′ĭ-ī) A member of the house of Saul who cursed King David as he fled from Jerusalem during Absalom's revolt. He ran along the top of a hill cursing and throwing stones at him. When David returned victorious, Shimei threw himself at David's feet and was forgiven. However, King David and his son Solomon never trusted Shimei again.

Shinar (shī′när) The ancient name for Babylonia.

Shiphrah (shĭf′rȧ) The name of one of the two midwives who disobeyed Pharaoh's orders to kill the male children born to the Israelite women. Because of this the infant Moses was spared. The other midwife was called Puah.

Shishak (shī′shăk) A Pharaoh of Egypt who invaded the Kingdom of Judah during the reign of Solomon's son Rehoboam. He plundered Jerusalem and took many of its treasures back to Egypt.

Shittim (shĭt′ĭm) The campsite of the Israelites between the end of their conquests east of the Jordan and their entrance into Canaan.

shittim wood The hard, yellow-brown wood of a certain tree which grew in Palestine. It was used in building the Tabernacle.

Shobi (shō′bī) An Ammonite who showed King David and his men great kindness when he fled across the Jordan during Absalom's revolt.

Shuhite (shōō′hīt) A name applied to Bildad, one of Job's three friends. It probably refers to the tribe to which he belonged.

Shunem (shōō′nĕm) A place 5 miles from Mount Tabor, where the Prophet Elisha was a guest in the home of a certain woman. He raised her young son from the dead.

Shushan (shōō′shăn) or **Susa** (sōō′sȧ) The capital of Persia in the days of Ahasuerus (Xerxes) and Artaxerxes. It was there that Queen Esther lived. Shushan was also the home of Nehemiah.

Sidon (sī′dȧn) and **Zidon** (zī′dȧn) A Phoenician city on the eastern coast of the Mediterranean north of Palestine. It was denounced by the Prophets Isaiah and Ezekiel and was visited by Jesus.

Sihon (sī′hŏn) King of the Amorites at the time the Israelites approached Canaan. He led a great force against them hoping to stop their advance, but was completely defeated.

Sihor (sī′hôr) or **Shihor** (shī′hôr) The name for the Nile used in the books of Isaiah and Jeremiah.

Silas (sī′lȧs) A prominent member of the Early Church in Jerusalem. He was also known as Silvanus, and accompanied Paul on his Second Missionary Journey.

Siloam (sĭ-lō′ȧm) A pool or reservoir in ancient Jerusalem. It was fed by a strong spring and was located southeast of the Temple mount.

Simeon (sĭm′ĭ-ȧn) 1. Jacob and Leah's second-born son. He was the founder of one of the Twelve Tribes of Israel.

2. The devout man who blessed the infant Jesus when Joseph and Mary brought Him to the Temple for His presentation to God. It had been revealed to Simeon that he would not die until he had seen

the Christ and he hailed the infant as the long-awaited Messiah.

Simon (sī'mȧn) There are many men named Simon who appear in the New Testament. The most important are the following: 1. Simon the Canaanite or Simon the Zealot, one of the Twelve Apostles.

2. Simon of Cyrene who carried the cross for Jesus.

3. Simon the Leper, a man of Bethany. It was at a feast at his home that Mary anointed Jesus.

4. Simon Magus, a Samaritan magician. He was converted to Christianity by Philip.

5. Simon Peter, the Apostle Peter.

6. Simon the tanner, a Christian convert at Joppa. A friend of Peter.

Sin (sĭn), **Wilderness of** A district between the Red Sea and Mount Sinai through which the Israelites passed. It was the place where God first sent them manna.

Sinai (sī'nī), **Mount** A mountain near the tip of the Sinai Peninsula. It was from the heights of Mount Sinai that Moses brought down the stone tablets inscribed with the Ten Commandments. It is sometimes called Mount Horeb.

Sion (sī'ȧn), **Mount** 1. One of the many names for Mount Hermon.

2. The Greek form of the Hebrew word Zion, the mount in Jerusalem on which the Temple stood.

Sisera (sĭs'ẽr-ȧ) Captain of the armies of the Canaanite king, Jabin. Sisera and his forces were defeated by Barak and Deborah at the River Kishon. After fleeing from the battlefield, Sisera was murdered by a woman who enticed him into her tent and then drove a nail into his head while he slept.

Smyrna (smẽr'nȧ) A city of Asia Minor located on the western shore of the Aegean Sea about 35 miles north of Ephesus. It was the site of one of the "seven churches of Asia."

Sodom (sŏd'ȧm) One of the "cities of the plain" which God destroyed because of the wickedness of their inhabitants. Lot and his wife and two daughters were, however, spared. In fleeing, Lot's wife disobeyed God's orders and looked back. For this she was turned into a pillar of salt.

Solomon

Solomon (sŏl'ō-m*a*n) One of King David's four sons by Bath-sheba. He became the third king of Israel and built the first Temple. It was a magnificent edifice, richly adorned and with roof beams hewn from the fragrant cedars of Lebanon. Solomon was renowned for his great wisdom.

Song of Solomon (sŏl'ō-m*a*n) or **Song of Songs** One of the poetical books of the Old Testament, said to have been written by Solomon about 1000 B.C. Most modern scholars, however, believe it was written much earlier.

spikenard (spīk'nĕrd) A very costly aromatic ointment with which Mary anointed Jesus as He sat at the feast in the home of Simon the Leper. In Biblical times spikenard was imported from Arabia, India and the Far East.

Stephanas (stĕf'*a*-năs) A Christian of Corinth. Paul baptized all the members of his household. They thus became "the firstfruits of Achaia" or "the firstfruits of Greece."

Stephen (stē'v*a*n) One of the seven deacons of the Early Christian Church in Jerusalem. He was stoned to death for his beliefs and thus became the first Christian martyr. Paul, who was then known as Saul, was present at the stoning and sided against Stephen and his Christian friends.

Succoth (sŭk'ŏth) 1. Succoth, meaning booth, was the name given to the place east of the Jordan where Jacob and his family camped after his reconciliation with his brother Esau. The place where Jacob built "booths" to shelter his family and his cattle.

2. The first camping site of the Israelites at the beginning of the Exodus.

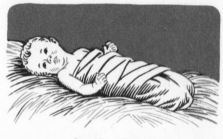

Swaddling Clothes

swaddling clothes Bands of cloth or clothes wrapped closely around a newborn child. According to the Gospel of Luke, the infant Jesus was wrapped in swaddling clothes before being placed in the manger.

synagogue (sĭn'*a*-gŏg) A word meaning "a gathering together" or "assembly." This term is applied to both the congregation and the building in which Jewish people hold their religious worship. Synagogues came into existence during the Babylonian Captivity. After the return to Palestine, however, the Jews continued their synagogues, and every city, town and hamlet seems to have had one. In spite of this the Temple in Jerusalem continued to be the focal point of Judaism. After the final destruction of the Temple and the Dispersion, the Jews centered their worship in their synagogues in whatever land they lived.

Syracuse (sĭr′a-kūs) An important and ancient city on the east coast of Sicily. Paul stopped there on his way to Rome.

Syria (sĭr′ĭ-a) A country often referred to in the Old and New Testaments. It was roughly 300 miles long and 50 to 150 miles wide and lay north and northeast of Palestine. Syria became a Roman province in 64 B.C. Damascus and Antioch were its main cities.

Tabernacle (tăb′ĕr-năk-l) "Tent of Jehovah" or "the dwelling place of God." An oblong tent of skin and cloth stretched over a wooden frame which served as a

Tabernacle

movable place of worship for the Israelites during the Wilderness wanderings. Moses brought detailed instructions for its building down from Mount Sinai. It was beautifully decorated and contained the Holy of Holies, which housed the sacred Ark of the Covenant. At each camping place during the 40 years of the wanderings, the Tabernacle was always carried in the center of all the Israelites with three tribes stationed or marching at each of its four sides. After the Israelites reached Canaan, the Tabernacle was located at Shiloh. It remained there until captured by the Philistines, together with the Ark of the Covenant. The Ark was finally returned and taken to Jerusalem by David. Solomon housed it in a magnificent Temple. After having been defiled by the Philistines, the Tabernacle lost its meaning to Israel and fell into oblivion. Its place was taken by the Temple.

Tabernacles (tăb′ĕr-năk-lz), **Feast of** The third of the three great yearly festivals of the Jews. It was instituted in Old Testament times and is still observed. It is a thanksgiving celebration held after the harvest and lasts for 7 days. It is named after the booths or "tabernacles" in which the people lived during the harvest.

Tabitha (tăb′ĭ-tha) A woman of

Joppa who was also known as Dorcas.

Tabor (tā'bĕr), **Mount** A solitary and isolated mountain that rises from the Valley of Jezreel, or Plain of Esdraelon, about 5 miles east of Nazareth. It is not mentioned in the New Testament but is referred to several times in the Old Testament. It was on Mount Tabor that Barak and Deborah assembled their forces in preparation for the battle against the Canaanites under Sisera which took place at the Kishon River.

Tadmor (tăd'môr) or **Tamar** (tā'mĕr) A fortified desert city built by Solomon west of the Euphrates and east of the city of Hamath.

talent (tăl'ant) In both the Old and New Testaments this term denotes a weight of money, not a coin. It was unminted precious metal and its value varied through the centuries. Silver talents were worth roughly 1,400 dollars and gold talents about 20,000 dollars in U. S. currency.

Tamar (tā'mĕr) 1. The wife, in succession, of Judah's two sons, Er and Onan.
2. The daughter of King David and Maachah. She was the full sister of Absalom. It was her great beauty that started the chain of tragic events which ended in Absalom's revolt and death.

tares A variety of weed which closely resembles wheat.

Tarshish (tär'shĭsh) A distant land, probably Spain, with which Solomon traded. It was to Tarshish that Jonah tried to flee to escape God's command that he preach repentance in Nineveh.

Tarsus (tär'sas) An important city of Cilicia in southern Asia Minor. Paul was born there.

Tekoa (tĭ-kō'a) A town in Judah about 6 miles south of Bethlehem. It was the scene of many Old Testament events. It is best known as the birthplace of the Prophet Amos and as the town from which Joab brought the "wise woman" to attempt a reconciliation between David and his beloved son Absalom.

Tema (tē'ma) Ishmael's ninth son. Grandson of Hagar and Abraham. He founded an Arabian tribe which bore his name. They were known as traders.

Teman (tē'man) The grandson of Esau and a member of a tribe which bore his name. These people lived somewhere in Edom. They were known for their great wisdom. One of Job's three friends was a Temanite.

Temple (tĕm'pl) To the ancient Jews of the Patriarchs and the Exodus, God was the only king and ruler. After settling in Canaan, they began to feel a need for an earthly ruler; thus Saul became their first king. However, God still retained an unrivaled position in the daily lives of the Jews. The Temple in Jerusalem which replaced the Tabernacle, or God's "dwelling place on earth," became the focal point of Judaic religious and political life.

Through the centuries, there have been three different and magnificent Temples.

1. Solomon's Temple, built by Solomon according to plans drawn by his father, King David. It lasted for 400 years, until razed by Nebuchadnezzar.

2. Zerubbabel's Temple, built when the Jews returned from their long Captivity in Babylonia. It was named after the man who devoted himself to its rebuilding. It lasted 500 years.

3. Herod's Temple. This was the Temple of Jesus' day. It was a remodeling and extension of Zerubbabel's Temple and covered almost 35 acres. It lasted only 90 years and was completely destroyed by the Romans under Titus in A.D. 70.

Ten Commandments The covenant between God and man which Moses brought down from Mount Sinai inscribed on two stone tablets. These Commandments are the fundamental laws of both the Jewish and Christian religions. They are also the basis of many of the civil laws of western civilization. The entire western way of life or moral code is deeply influenced by them.

Terah (tē'rȧ) The father of Abraham, Nahor and Haran. As an old man he left his home in Ur of the Chaldees and with Abraham and his people started in search of a new home in Canaan. However, he did not reach Canaan but died on the way, in Haran.

teraphim (tĕr'ȧ-fĭm) Images or statuettes of pagan gods connected with magical rites. They are mentioned several times in the Old Testament. Rachel took the teraphim from her father's house when her husband, Jacob, moved back to Canaan with all his household and flocks.

Teraphim

Tertius (tẽr'shĭ-ȧs) The scribe or secretary who wrote out Paul's Epistle to the Romans. He was probably a Roman.

Tertullus (tẽr-tŭl'ȧs) "A certain orator," probably a Roman, who accused Paul before the Roman procurator Felix at Caesarea.

testament (tĕs′ta-mănt) A solemn agreement or covenant between two or more persons. The Bible consists of two main parts, the Old Testament and the New Testament. The Old Testament is the "old" or "first" agreement between God and man. The New Testament is the "new" or "second" agreement between God and man.

tetrach (tĕt′rärk) The title used for anyone who ruled a Roman province. As a courtesy tetrachs were sometimes addressed as "king."

Thaddaeus (thă-dē′as) One of the Twelve Apostles. He is believed to be the same person as Jude and Lebbaeus.

Thebez (thē′bĕz) A town near Shechem where Gideon's evil son Abimelech died. While storming this place with his forces he was hit on the head by a woman with a piece of millstone. Fearing that it would be said that a woman had killed him, he asked his soldiers to slay him.

Theophilus (thĭ-ŏf′ĭ-las) The man to whom the Gospel of Luke and The Acts are inscribed. He was a Gentile of high position. When he came under the influence of Luke and Paul in Rome, he became a Christian convert.

Thessalonians (thĕs-a-lō′nĭ-anz), **First and Second** Two New Testament epistles, or letters, written by Paul from Corinth to the new church in Thessalonica.

Thessalonica (thĕs-a-lō-nī′ka) The capital of Macedonia, where Paul founded one of the first Christian churches. He was later forced to leave this city because his enemies started a riot against him.

Thieves, The Two Two thieves were crucified with Jesus. Their crosses stood on either side of His.

Thomas (tŏm′as) One of the Twelve Apostles. He is known as "doubting Thomas" because he would not believe in the Resurrection until Jesus appeared before him and showed him His wounds. He is also known as Didymus.

Thyatira (thī-a-tī′ra) An ancient city in Lydia in Asia Minor. It was the home of Paul's hostess Lydia, and was the site of one of the "seven churches of Asia."

Tiberias (tī-bē′rĭ-ăs) A city on the western shore of the Sea of Galilee. It was built by Herod Antipas as his capital and named in honor of the Roman Emperor Tiberius.

Tiglath–pileser (tĭg′lăth=pĭ-lē′zĕr) A warring Assyrian king who helped King Ahaz of Judah against King Pekah of the Northern Kingdom. As a result of this, Ahaz became a vassal of Tiglath-pileser.

Tigris (tī'grĭs) A great river, which together with the Euphrates, rises in the Armenian mountains and flows southeast to empty into the Persian Gulf. It was one of the rivers of Eden.

timbrel (tĭm'brắl) or **tabret** (tăb'rĕt) A musical instrument closely resembling the modern tambourine. In Bible times it was usually played by women or young girls and was used as an accompaniment to singing and dancing.

Timbrel

Timnath–serah (tĭm'nắth=sē'rắ) A city given to Joshua by the Children of Israel and near which he was buried. It was about 9 miles south of Shechem.

Timothy (tĭm'ō-thĭ) The young friend and companion of Paul. His father was Greek and his mother was Jewish. Their home was in either Lystra or Derbe in central Asia Minor. He was taught the Holy Scriptures by his very devout mother, Eunice, and his equally devout grandmother, Lois.

Timothy (tĭm'ō-thĭ), **First and Second** These two epistles of the New Testament are letters of instruction written by Paul to his young friend and assistant.

Tirshatha (tĕr-shā'thắ) The title given to the Hebrew governors of Judah during the Persian domination.

Tirzah (tĕr'zắ) An ancient Canaanite city captured by the Israelites when they entered the Promised Land. Several centuries later it became the royal city of Jeroboam, first king of the Northern Kingdom. The beauty of Tirzah was well-known and is mentioned in the Song of Solomon.

Tishbite (tĭsh'bīt) The name by which the Prophet Elijah was often called.

tithe A tenth part of all earnings from labor, land or livestock dedicated to God. This practice has existed from earliest Biblical times and is first recorded in Genesis.

Titus (tī'tắs) 1. A companion and assistant of Paul. He was a Greek by birth and was converted by Paul. The Epistle to Titus, one of the books of the New Testament, was written by Paul to this young man.

2. A man at whose home in

Corinth Paul preached; his surname was Justus.

Tobiah (tō-bī′à) An Ammonite who joined Sanballat, the Samaritan, in opposing Nehemiah's work of rebuilding the walls of Jerusalem.

tongues, gift of The gift which the Holy Spirit gave to the disciples on the Day of Pentecost in Jerusalem following the Ascension. Those who were from distant lands and who spoke only in foreign tongues miraculously heard everything in their own languages.

Tophet (tō′fĕt) A place in the abominable Valley of Hinnom south of Jerusalem. This was a pagan center of worship for the fire-god Molech. It was defiled for Israel by King Josiah who littered it with bones and all kinds of filth.

tribute (trĭb′ūt) 1. A Temple tribute or tax of a half shekel was paid by all Jews for the upkeep of the Temple.
2. Crushing taxes or tributes were extracted from the Jews in New Testament times by the Roman conquerors.

Tubal (tū′bàl) A son of Japheth and grandson of Noah. He was the probable founder of a tribe of traders who lived near the Black Sea.

Tyre (tīr) A Phoenician city on the Mediterranean just south of Sidon and north of Palestine. Hiram, king of Tyre, sent skilled workmen and materials to his friends King David and King Solomon for the building of the palace and the first Temple in Jerusalem. Centuries later Jesus visited Tyre and Sidon.

Ur (ĕr) The land of Haran's birth and the place from which Terah and his son Abraham and his people started out for Canaan. It is generally believed that Ur was situated in Chaldea not far from where the Euphrates and Tigris Rivers join and flow into the Persian Gulf.

Uriah (ū-rī′à) An officer in King David's army and the husband of Bath-sheba. David had him sent into a very dangerous part of the battlefield, where he was killed. David then married Bath-sheba. She became the mother of several of his children, including Solomon.

Urijah (ū-rī′jà) 1. High Priest in the days of Ahaz, king of Judah.
2. A minor prophet of Judah who, like Jeremiah, rebuked King Jehoiakim and foretold the destruction of Jerusalem.

Urim (ū′rĭm) and **Thummim** (thŭm′ĭm) Two mysterious and unidentified objects worn by the High Priest over his heart and under his breastplate. They seem to have been consulted when, under special circumstances, the priest wanted advice from God.

Uz (ŭz) The land where Job lived. It was probably situated east or southeast of Palestine, near Chaldea.

Uzzah (ŭz'á) or **Uzza** (ŭz'á) One of the sons of Abinadab, in whose home the Ark of the Covenant rested for twenty years. When David was moving the Ark to Jerusalem on an oxcart, it slipped and Uzzah caught it to prevent it from falling to the ground. He was immediately struck dead by heaven for having thus profaned its holiness.

Uzziah (ŭ-zī'á) The son of King Amaziah of Judah. When he was 16, he was chosen as king by the people following his father's murder. He reigned for 52 years and proved to be a wise and pious man, deeply influenced by the Prophet Zechariah. Uzziah, however, faltered toward the end of his life; he tried to force the Temple priests to let him burn incense at the holy altar. For this he was suddenly stricken with leprosy.

Vashti (văsh'tī) The queen of Persia. She was deposed for disobeying her husband, King Ahasuerus (Xerxes); he wanted her to appear at a feast before his friends and visiting princes. Esther was then chosen by Ahasuerus as his new queen.

Veil of the Tabernacle and Temple A very fine linen curtain of blue, purple and scarlet woven with figures of cherubim. It hung from four pillars dividing the Tabernacle into two compartments. These were the Holy Place and the Holy of Holies. The Holy Place contained the golden seven-branched candlestick, the altar of incense and the shewbread. The Holy of Holies contained the Ark of the Covenant.

Veil of the Tabernacle

vinegar (vĭn'ĭ-gẽr) The Biblical term used for wine or other strong drinks which had turned sour. These were used by laborers. A similar drink diluted with water was used by Roman soldiers. This was probably the drink that was offered to Jesus in his dying moments on the cross.

Vineyards (vĭn'yĕrds), **Plain of the** A district lying at the northeast end of the Dead Sea, east of the Jordan.

W **wafers** (wā'fẽrz) Thin unleavened cakes made of flour. Honey was sometimes added as a sweetening. These cakes, rubbed with oil, were used in numerous Hebrew religious services.

whale The "whales" mentioned in the Bible were probably any very large fish, such as the dolphin or shark, which inhabited the waters of the Mediterranean. This term does not refer to the true whales of the Atlantic and Pacific Oceans.

wilderness (wĭl'dẽr-nĕs) In Biblical times Palestine and the surrounding territory had many large desert areas which had sparse vegetation only during certain rainy seasons. There are many references to the Wilderness in both the Old and New Testaments. The Children of Israel wandered for 40 years through the Wilderness after escaping from bondage in Egypt. John the Baptist and Jesus spent days of contemplation in the Wilderness.

Wise Men Certain men or scholars who were deeply versed in spiritual and practical truths, such as astronomy. They were greatly revered by the people and were classed together with priests and prophets. The Wise Men or Magi, who came from the distant East to worship the infant Jesus, belonged to this group. They are also believed to have been kings or priests.

witch and **witchcraft** (wĭch'krăft) Sorcery, or witchcraft, was forbidden on pain of death to the people of Israel; it was considered an abomination in the eyes of God. However, it existed. We read in the Old Testament that King Saul consulted the witch of En-dor on the evening before the fateful battle of Gilboa. The evil Queen Jezebel and Manasseh, king of Judah, both encouraged witches. Two witches or magicians mentioned in the New Testament are Simon Magus of Samaria and Bar-Jesus, a friend of Sergius Paulus, Roman proconsul of Cyprus.

wormwood (wẽrm'wōŏd) A plant from which a bitter juice can be extracted. Several varieties of it grow in Palestine. The term "wormwood" is used as a symbol for "bitter" or "unfortunate" experience. In Amos we read, "Ye who turn judgment to wormwood, and leave off righteousness in the earth." In Jeremiah we read "I will feed them . . . with wormwood, and give them water of gall to drink."

Yoke

yoke A heavy wooden crosspiece for joining two oxen or other animals. In the Bible this term is used as a symbol of subjection or to denote a burden. Jesus offered to lighten man's "burden" or "yoke."

Zabud (zā′bŭd) Son of the Prophet Nathan. He was a priest and served as "principal officer, and the king's friend" in Solomon's court.

Zacchaeus (ză-kē′ăs) A wealthy publican and tax collector near Jericho who, being short in stature, climbed into a sycamore tree so that he might see Jesus as He passed with His disciples. Jesus noticed him, spoke to him and went with him to his home.

Zacharias (zăk-a-rī′ăs) The husband of Elisabeth and father of John the Baptist. He was a priest. An angel appeared to him while he was in the Temple and announced to him the coming birth of his son.

Zadok (zā′dŏk) One of two High Priests in King David's reign. He was always deeply devoted to David. When David and his men fled from Jerusalem during Absalom's revolt, Zadok accompanied him, carrying along the sacred Ark of the Covenant.

Zalmunna (zăl-mŭn′na) One of the two Midianite kings slain by Gideon. The other one was Zebah.

Zaphnath–paaneah (zăf′năth=pā-a-nē′a) The Egyptian name given to Joseph by Pharaoh. It meant "said God, he lives."

Zarephath (zăr′ĭ-făth) A Phoenician city about 8 miles south of Sidon. The Prophet Elijah lived there in the widow's house toward the end of a great drought and famine which covered the land.

Zaretan (zăr′ĭ-tăn) or **Zartanah** (zär-ta′na) or **Zarthan** (zär′thăn) A village in the Jordan Valley below Jezreel, not far from the city of Beth-shean. The bronze castings for Solomon's Temple were made there.

Zebah (zē′ba) One of the two Midianite kings who invaded Palestine with a great force which was defeated by Gideon. He captured the two kings and, taking them to his home at Ophrah, he killed them. Oreb and Zeeb were among this Midianite horde.

Zebedee (zĕb'ĭ-dē) The father of the two apostles James and John and the husband of Salome, their mother and one of Jesus' most devoted disciples.

Zeboim (zĭ-bō'ĭm) One of the "cities of the plain" that God destroyed because of the wickedness of the inhabitants.

Zebudah (zĭ-bū'dȧ) The wife of King Josiah of Judah and the mother of King Jehoiakim.

Zebul (zē'bŭl) Chief of the city of Shechem in the days of King Abimelech of Shechem, the son of Gideon. Zebul helped to put down an insurrection which took place during Abimelech's absence.

Zebulun (zĕb'ū-lȧn) Jacob and Leah's sixth son. A founder of one of the Twelve Tribes of Israel.

Zechariah (zĕk-ȧ-rī'ȧ) or **Zachariah** (zăk-ȧ-rī'ȧ) 1. The last king of the Jehu dynasty of the Northern Kingdom. He was the son of King Jeroboam II and reigned only six months before being murdered by Shallum, who then seized the throne.

2. A priest and minor Hebrew prophet. He was born in Babylonia during the Captivity and went to Jerusalem when the Israelites were finally freed from bondage in the foreign land. He devoted himself to the rebuilding of the Temple. His words and visions are recorded in the Old Testament book which bears his name.

3. Son of the High Priest Jehoiada during the reign of King Joash of Judah. He fought the worship of pagan gods and was stoned to death in the Temple court as the result of a plot which had been formed against him by the king. He is probably the "Zacharias son of Barachias" mentioned in the Gospel of Matthew.

Zedekiah (zĕd-ĭ-kī'ȧ) A son of King Josiah of Judah. After his father's death he was placed on the throne by Nebuchadnezzar and his real name, Mattaniah, was changed to Zedekiah. Shortly after this he led an unsuccessful rebellion against the Babylonian conquerors. Jerusalem and the Temple were then destroyed. At Nebuchadnezzar's orders Zedekiah was blinded and led with his people into captivity in Babylonia.

Zeeb (zē'ĕb) One of the two Midianite princes, Oreb and Zeeb, who were slain during the Midian invasion of Palestine. Zeeb means "wolf."

Zelophehad (zĭ-lō'fĭ-hăd) A man of the Tribe of Manasseh. He died during the Wilderness wanderings and his five daughters went before Moses to claim his inheritance. He had no male heirs. Their claims were finally recognized through divine intervention.

Zephaniah (zĕf-à-nī′à) 1. A minor prophet of Israel whose words are contained in the Old Testament book which bears his name. He lived during the reign of Josiah, king of Judah.

2. A Temple priest during the reign of Zedekiah, king of Judah. He was captured when Jerusalem was razed and taken to Nebuchadnezzar at Riblah, where he was slain.

Zerah (zē′rà) An Ethiopian prince or king who invaded Palestine during the reign of Asa, the third king of Judah. Although his army was very well equipped and numbered a "million" men, it was quickly defeated.

Zerubbabel (zà-rŭb′à-bàl) A man born during the Babylonian Captivity. When Cyrus became king of Persia and released the Jews from the Captivity, Zerubbabel was leader of one of the groups of returning exiles. After reaching Jerusalem, he immediately started the rebuilding of the Temple.

Ziba (zī′bà) One of Saul's servants, whom David turned over to Saul's son Mephibosheth. During Absalom's revolt, he falsely accused his master of planning to seize the throne. David believed him and gave him all of Mephibosheth's estates. David, however, learned the truth upon his return to Jerusalem and so the properties were given back to Mephibosheth.

Ziklag (zĭk′lăg) A town given to David by the Philistine king of Gath as a refuge from Saul. David lived there for a year and four months or until he learned of King Saul's death.

Zilpah (zĭl′pà) Leah's Syrian handmaid. She bore Jacob two sons, Gad and Asher.

Zimri (zĭm′rī) An officer in the army of the Northern Kingdom. He murdered King Elah and seized the throne, thus becoming the fifth king of the Northern Kingdom. However, he reigned only 7 days before being deposed by Omri, another army officer. Omri was then proclaimed king.

Zin (zĭn), **Wilderness of** A desert tract lying directly southwest of the Dead Sea. The Israelites wandered through this land on their way from Egypt to Canaan.

Zion (zī′àn) One of the hills of Jerusalem. The Temple stood on Mount Zion.

Ziph (zĭf), **Wilderness of** A wild,

hilly district of Judah where David hid from Saul.

Zipporah (zĭ-pō'rȧ) The daughter of Jethro, a Midianite priest. She married Moses and became the mother of his two sons Gershom and Eliezer.

Zoan (zō'ăn) An ancient city of lower Egypt. It is mentioned in Psalm 78 as having been the site of the plagues which God visited upon the Egyptians.

Zoar (zō'ẽr) One of the most ancient cities of Canaan. It was the "city of the plain" which God spared as a shelter for Lot and his family when He destroyed Sodom and the others.

Zoba (zō'bȧ) or **Zobah** (zō'bȧ) A part of Syria which was at one time an independent kingdom. Zoba was often at war with its neighbors, including Israel, under David and Solomon.

Zophar (zō'fẽr) One of Job's three friends.

Zorah (zō'rȧ) A town in Judah. It was Samson's home, and his body was carried from Gaza to a spot near Zorah for burial.